RURAL STORY BOOK

Memories and Fabrications

by

Lance J. Clough

DORRANCE
PUBLISHING CO
EST. 1920
PITTSBURGH, PENNSYLVANIA 15238

Dorrance Publishing Co
585 Alpha Drive
Suite 103
Pittsburgh, PA 15238
Visit our website at *www.dorrancebookstore.com*

ISBN: 979-8-88729-142-0
eISBN: 979-8-88729-642-5

This book is dedicated to Debbie Aloisi and Brian Larington. Debbie helped by editing the individual stories and Brian by providing the cover art.

RURAL STORY BOOK

MEMORIES AND FABRICATIONS

DOWNHILL RUN

Christmas vacation always seemed to bring at least one snowstorm along with it. This year was no exception. The storm slinked slowly across the country seemingly blanketing each Midwestern town in its path over the earth's surface from the upper boundaries of Northwestern Canada to the Ohio River Valley and eastward.

A heavy blanket of fresh snow is an irresistible phenomena to children and adults alike. Many a house yard was an exciting family play land as young and old joined in to transform the yards into snow-families, sled slides, or some form of winter recreation.

Jerry and Jay woke up to just such a surprise one vacation morn.

"Jerry," said Jay, "get up! We're supposed to go sledding with the Folgen brothers this morning. At least that's what Jared Folgen told me last night. They'll be sledding down the hill north of the county road Jared told me."

"What do you mean, Jay? We're supposed to go sledding with Jared and Nick?" replied Jerry. "Did Jared or Nick ask you if you wanted to go along with them?"

"Kinda," said Jay as he began dressing in his outdoor winter clothes. "Jared told me yesterday that he and Nick were going sledding down the big hill across the county road. I said could Jerry and I go with you?"

"So, you begged him, did you, little brother?" asked Jerry almost making a statement instead of waiting for an answer. Jay would begin school next year so he was "Little Brother" yet to Jerry.

"I asked him and he said it was okay, so it is!" Jay added rather to the point.

"Has the hill been packed yet?" asked Jerry as he, too, hurried to pull on his winter clothes.

"I don't know," said Jay as he finished dressing. "We can help with that this morning." He ran across the bedroom, down the stairs and into the shoe and boot closet under the stairs.

"Wait a minute!" said their mother to a startled Jay as he lost his balance from the start Mother had given him.

"You scared me, Mom," said Jay as he tried to pick himself up off the floor not letting go of his right shoe. *PLOP* went Jay again as he repeated his last stunt.

"Be careful around me today, Jerry," mused Jay as he finally got back up and put on his right shoe and soon followed it by his left shoe.

"Are you going outside without breakfast, Jay?" asked Mother, knowing, since she mentioned breakfast, Jay would not be able to skip it.

"Are you up this early, Mom?" asked Jerry, believing he was an early bird.

"It is not early anymore, son. Your father is out of here every morning at five-forty-five," replied Mother.

"What time is it?" asked Jay even though he would have little or no idea what the answer his request yielded would mean.

"You can't tell time anyway," injected Jerry as he sped past Jay and grabbed his coat.

"Just you wait a minute, young men!" demanded Mother. "You both better have breakfast before you go out gallivanting all over the countryside."

"Okay, Mom," said Jay, turning to face Jerry. "Huh! So there! You thought you'd get outside ahead of me! Now you have 'ta wait with me."

"We'll have breakfast; then we can stay out until dinnertime," assured Jerry as he looked cross-eyed at Jay.

Mother made pancakes for the boys as she asked them where they would be sledding.

"Jay said Jared kinda asked him to go sledding with him and Nick this morning, Mom," Jerry explained. "Jay said they would be sledding down the big hill road that meets the county road from the north."

"Be careful, boys! The county road may have traffic on it. Make sure your little brother keeps up with everyone too," Mom delegated to Jerry as Jerry scratched his head wondering if somewhere in Mom's statement, he had a duty to do something. Jerry and Jay felt safe because the county road seldom had traffic on it even in the morning.

"What are you asking, Mom?" asked Jerry still a little bewildered.

"Jerry, I am asking you to watch out for your little brother today so he doesn't get hurt! He is much smaller than you, so it is your job to look out for him!"

Unknown to Jerry or anyone else, this constant asking of Jerry to look out for his "little brother" is what gave Jay the nickname of "Little Brother."

"I'm kinda hungry, Mom," said Jay, thinking he was now ready for breakfast.

"Jay!" said Mother rather abruptly. "Wash your hands before you eat."

"Yes, Mom," answered Jay as he slid a stool to the kitchen counter, got hold of the water dipper and slowly and methodically dipped water from the pail on the counter and into the wash basin that sat alone in the sink. Splash went the water as it hit the bottom of the empty basin.

"Careful, Jay or you will have my whole kitchen wet. You're supposed to wash your hands not my kitchen! Jerry—"

"Yes, Mom, I know," said Jerry as he helped Jay get water ready for Jay to wash his hands for breakfast. "I need to help my little brother."

"Thank you, Jerry," sighed Mom, continuing to make breakfast pancakes. "Jay is little and needs a big brother like you that he can look up to for help." Jay got his hands wet and soapy with Jerry's help and soon had his hands washed and rinsed. "You can help your brother too, Jay," said Mother as she watched her boys out of the corner of her eyes.

"I don't need help from a little boy, Mother. I can do it myself!" said Jerry cockily.

"Okay, Jerry," said Mother, finishing the cakes. "I got your plates down. You just have to get out the milk, jam, margarine, and forks to have with your cakes, Jerry," Mother said as she looked pleadingly at Jerry, hoping that he wouldn't think he was doing too much so early in the morning. Dad got butter. The rest of the family got margarine as a spread. Jay just had jam. He would not eat margarine.

"Jay! Wipe your mouth before the jam…falls…on…." Mother's voice trailed off and she saw Jay lift the sleeve of his shirt level with his mouth and quickly wipe it across his face before she could protest.

"Jay! After breakfast you'll need to change your shirt. You just got jam all over your sleeve," said Mother in a scolding voice.

"Ain't he a mess!" laughed Jerry softly to himself while he ate cakes and drank his milk. "Little brothers are fun, Mom," stated Jerry with a mouth full of cakes and jam.

"Careful, Jerry or you'll have jam all over you too."

"Where do I have jam?"

"Nowhere yet," scolded their mother. "But you are not immune from messes, either!"

Jerry and Jay finished their breakfasting, changed any soiled outer clothing and went under the stairway and got their winter outer wear. Mother sewed all of their outer clothing and some under clothing as well, so the family could afford dressing all of the children properly for each season of the year. Other mothers in the area did the same. Clothes were never thrown away, but given to others or traded for better fitting clothing as children grew. Hand-me-downs were the consequence of being a younger sibling. When clothing was too worn to wear, it would be found in someone's next year's quilt.

"Jay! You're putting on my snowsuit!" yelled Jerry at a confused Jay.

"I made you a new snowsuit yesterday, Jerry. Jay needs to wear your old one this winter. I patched it so it would last another year. You were hard on your snowsuit last winter, Jerry," explained Mother, helping to keep the boys from quarreling. "By the way, Jerry," continued Mother, "I also got you new boots. Jay will wear your old boots."

"But my old boots had leaks in the sides, Mother," confessed Jerry while he began pulling on his new boots.

"Father put inner-tube patches on your old boots so they are fine for another season for Jay," Mother further explained.

"You got my old clothes and boots, Jay," teased Jerry as he finished getting ready for outside.

"I don't mind, Jerry. At least I get to go out and play" was all Jay cared about at that moment. Away they went out the door, down the length of the driveway, up the hill, and to the neighbors.

"Are Jared or Nick here?" asked Jerry, bursting through the neighbor's front door after receiving permission to enter.

"No. Jared went sledding on the hill above the county road," said their mother matter-of-factly. "Nick had to work with his father."

"Thank you," said Jerry politely as he shut the door and went back to where Jay was standing by their sleds. (The older girls got sleds one year for Christmas and the boys got sleds the following year.)

The neighbor's house was on top of a hill too. Just not as large a hill as the one that ran down to the county road from the north. The brothers bent over, grabbed their sleds, ran about ten feet and jumped onto the top of their sleds as they made their way down the hill that met the county road from the south. Once at the bottom, they walked across the county road and to the road that ran steeply up the side of the big hill to the north, which was their goal.

"Hey!" screamed Jared down the hill to the boys at the bottom as he went sledding down the hill past Jerry and Jay. Jared hit the snowbank purposefully at the bottom of the hill so he would avoid crossing the county roadway. "Are you two sledding with me today?"

"Yes!" exclaimed Jerry walking to Jared. "We planned on sledding all morning. Where is Nick?"

"Nick had chores to do for Dad so he won't be here today. Did you notice that the hill got plowed, Jay?" asked Jared, motioning towards the hill he just slid down.

"Yah, Jared. I did see that. Who did it?" said Jay as he puzzled over the neat job of plowing someone had done.

"Mr. Chester plowed the hill with the town grader early this morning. Dad asked him to plow so all of the neighborhood kids could go sledding down it," explained Jared to two happy boys. "We need to go back up the hill and slide down," finished Jared, so, back up he went with two younger boys trailing behind him.

Mr. Chester did a great job of plowing. He did not scrape the hill down to bare gravel and grass as someone who didn't understand the purpose of the plowing might have done. Since Mr. Chester knew it was for children to slide down, he left a couple of inches of snow for sledding. The snow below the grader's blade was also packed into a hard almost ice-like surface. The hill had a long downhill run, had a hump in it, and went back to a downhill slope. This hump is what made it so much fun for boys and girls. The hump sometimes made sleds go airborne for a brief time, though each boy believed his sled alone flew for a while.

Up the hill climbed the boys, pulling their sleds behind them. "I have been down this hill three times already," said Jared, helping Jay untangle himself from his sled rope.

"Thanks, Jared!" said Jay since he was now able to walk faster and nearly kept up with the other two older boys. "I am going to be the fastest sledder today!" challenged Jay with a smile.

"What makes you think that?" asked Jared.

"Grandpa waxed my sled runners yesterday. He says wax will help my sled be faster in cold weather," Jay said proudly as he tripped on his sled rope and almost fell again. Jared caught him just in time.

"Be careful, Jared," warned Jerry with a grin. "Jay almost killed himself at home, too, this morning by falling over two times as he tried to put his shoes on. It was a fun sight to see!"

"I couldn't help it!" said Jay in his own defense. "Mom scared me!"

"She scared you the first time, Jay, but you fell over a second time too," laughed Jerry as they all reached the top of the hill. All three of them scanned the scenery as they looked from right to left at the valley below.

"Wow!" said Jay quietly. "I never saw so much white snow before!"

"What color was the other snow you saw, Jay?" teased Jerry.

"I mean I never saw it from above. Looks like there's more of it from up here," explained Jay.

"Before you slide down the hill," explained Jared, "you need to follow a few rules. Before you begin to slide down the hill, wait until the one before you reaches that small evergreen tree a little way down the hill. Do you see it just down a bit?" asked Jared as he pointed down a poor bit of treetop alone and cold-looking as it rose barely above the snow around it.

"Yes, I see it," chimed Jerry and Jay, not quite sure the small bit of a tree to be barely seen above the surrounding snow was what Jared meant.

"Okay," said Jared as he continued. "After the guy ahead of you reaches the tree, it is okay for you to start down the hill. I don't want any accidents today 'cause I will catch heck if anything happens to either one of you."

"Why will you catch heck if we get hurt?" asked Jerry with a look of disbelief showing on his face.

"I will catch heck because I am the oldest and your parents and mine will expect me to watch out for you since you are younger."

"That doesn't sound right, Jared," said Jerry as he looked puzzled for a while. "Oh! I got it!" Jerry continued. "It's just like me when Jay and me go somewhere. I am supposed to watch out for him because I am older."

"Yup!" said Jared. "It's the same thing. Older people are supposed to help out younger people. So you understand what I mean by waiting before you begin to slide after someone?"

"Yup!" both younger boys said in reply.

"There's another thing too," said Jared. "Before you get all the way down the hill, you need to turn into the left bank made by the edge of the plow when Mr. Chester plowed down the hill. I will go down the farthest. You two hit the snowbank uphill from me."

The boys nodded in agreement whether they understood or not. Jared picked up his sled, ran about ten feet and quickly bent over, put his sled down on the plowed road and jumped onto his sled and was on his way downhill. Jerry waited until Jared got to the agreed-on tree and he, too, ran about ten feet and jumped onto his sled. Jay did the same as soon as Jerry got to the small evergreen tree. The hill was about a quarter mile long and dropped about two hundred or more feet in its descent. It afforded a swift if not too long a ride for the boys. Snow flew as

Jared turned into the ridge of snow at the road's edge and looked back at the two neighbor boys sledding behind him. A patch of white rose up as Jerry, too, hit the bank of snow.

All Jay saw was a cloud of fluffy snow in the air as he sailed past Jerry first and then Jared, "Whoa!" yelled Jay as he felt pressure on his left boot and then felt weightless. He landed hard on his belly and on the old road as all three boys saw his sled continue down the hill and proceed across the county road and into the path of the oncoming milk truck. The truck made an every-other-day stop at the farmers in the area to pick up their milk and take it to a creamery where many different types of dairy products were made from it. Jay's sled ran under the truck ahead of the back dual wheels of the truck and reemerged out the back of the truck between the dual wheels.

"Are you all right, Jay?" asked Jared as he watched the path of the truck.

"Wow, Jay!" exclaimed Jerry as he, too, watched Jay's sled as it emerged out of the back of the truck.

"Did you see that?" Jay shouted out at Jerry and Jared.

"Yes, we did, Jay," said Jared. "Why didn't you hit the snowbank as I told you?" Jared was a bit upset as he finally realized that the sledding would have ended quite badly had he not instinctively grabbed Jay's booted foot and pulled him off his sled as he went past.

"Yeah, Jay," added Jerry. "Why didn't you hit the bank next to me?"

"I was having so much fun sliding downhill that I must a forgot to hit the bank. And besides, all I saw of you two was a cloud of white powder in the air." That was Jay's only defense for his potentially dangerous mistake.

"Jared probably saved your life, Jay," said Jerry, dusting the snow powder off his pants. "Are you okay, Jay?" asked Jerry finally concerned about his little brother.

"I'm okay, Jerry," answered Jay as he finally realized, too, that he may have been run over by the truck just because he did not obey the instructions given to him by Jared. He also realized that Jared gave him rules so he would be safe as he enjoyed sliding down the hill.

"Wait, Jay!" said Jared, watching Jay head for the county road to retrieve his sled. "I will go with you so I'm sure you don't get run over by something."

"You worry too much about me," said Jay as he turned to step onto the edge of the road only to be stopped by Jared as yet another vehicle drove past the boys and swerved to miss Jay.

This time Jared was not as nice as he was before as he talked to Jay about rules and looking both ways before crossing the roadway. Jay's sled was brought back to the other side of the road by Jared. "Do we still feel like sledding?" asked Jared of the boys as he sat down on his sled, looking a bit pale.

"Yeah, we do," said Jerry as he sat down on his sled beside Jared.

"Golly. I'm sorry, Jared," said Jay as he, too, sat on his sled. "I'll be more careful before anything from now on."

"Okay," answered Jared as he got up off his sled and began to climb back up the hill so he could slide down again.

The rest of the morning's sledding went fine since Jay paid attention to his surroundings before proceeding forward and he went down the hill right after Jared. As the boys went home, Jay asked Jerry, "Please don't tell Mom about my almost getting run over by a milk truck, Jerry. She'll probably scold me if you do."

"I won't, Jay," answered Jerry as he realized Jay was worried that Mom would probably not allow him to slide down the same hill again this winter. Jerry and Jay slowly walked home from the neighbor's since Jared went inside his house and left them to walk home together.

"Hi, Mom," said the boys as they entered their house and began dropping their now wet snowsuits on the floor where they fell.

"Wait a minute, boys!" hastened Mother as she checked them over from head to toe. "Your clothes are too wet to put on the floor. You will need to hang them on the wet clothes rack," Mother told them. The wet clothes rack was a wooden fold out rack used for drying damp clothes in inclement weather.

Slowly the boys undressed and carefully they hung their wet clothes on the drying rack. They knew if they wanted to have sledding fun over this Christmas vacation time, they better pay attention to Mom.

"Did you have fun sledding today?" asked a patient mother.

"Yes, we did, Mother," replied Jerry as he winked at Jay to show Jay that he would not tell their mother anything that would get him into trouble.

"We went down the hill many times," said Jay as his excitement grew. "The road had been plowed by Mr. Chester, Mom."

"I wonder how he plowed it," stated Mother more to herself than to the boys.

"He used the town grader, Mom. Jared said his dad asked Mr. Chester to plow the hill so many of the neighborhood children could slide down it over Christmas vacation," finished Jerry.

"That was nice of Mr. Folgen to remember all you children at this time," replied Mother as she made lunch for the boys and herself.

"Where are our sisters?" asked Jay as he looked around the house.

"They were asked to babysit for the five children of the new neighbors down the road. It seems that Mrs. Folgen mentioned to them that our girls would babysit at times. Wasn't that nice of Mrs. Folgen to mention your sisters for babysitting?"

"We had so much fun, Mom," said Jay barely able to catch his breath. "We slid down and hit the bank so we wouldn't cross the road on our sleds," continued Jay.

"We had to let the person ahead of us get part-way down the hill before we could begin down the hill," added Jerry.

"And I almost got run over by a truck!" Jay blurted in his excitement forgetting not to tell on himself.

"What happened?" asked Mother, turning to listen to the boys and momentarily stopping her work to listen.

"I better tell you, Mom, or Jay will get himself into trouble," volunteered Jerry. "Jared told us to run our sleds into the snowbank at the left side of the plowed road so we wouldn't go across the county road. He went down first and I followed him. I hit the bank on the uphill side of Jared. When Jay came down last he said all he saw was a cloud of fluffy snow in the air around us so he continued down the hill past me and past Jared. Well, when he went past Jared, Jared just grabbed Jay's foot and pulled him off his sled."

"It happened so fast, Mom, that I didn't even know he did it until I hit the road with my belly," added Jay.

"Well, Mom, Jay's sled continued down the rest of the hill and across the roadway right under the milk truck."

"Oh, no!" cried Mother as she imagined Jay getting run over by the truck. "You have to be more careful, Jay. Are you all right?"

"I am fine, Mom," answered Jay.

"He's okay, Mom," continued Jerry as he told the rest of the story. "Jay's sled ran under the side of the milk truck between the front and back tires and came out between the two rear tires. Jared probably saved Jay's life," added Jerry.

"Jay, you have to pay way more attention to rules if you want to continue to be allowed to play with older children."

"It went so fast, Mom, I couldn't see who was where when I got to the bottom of the hill," interrupted a worried Jay as he felt the conversation getting out of hand.

"I know that confusing events can go wrong, son, but at some point you have to be paying attention or you may pay too dearly someday. You need to learn from this. It is important."

Jay learned that day that rules were for our own safety, not to get in the way of our fun.

"We also changed our order of sledding, Mom," added Jerry. "Jay went right after Jared and hit the bank on the upside of Jared and I went down last and hit the bank on the upside of Jay," finished Jerry.

A DAY AT SCHOOL

As the pealing of the bell signaling the beginning of school carried down into the valley, two brothers took action.

"Here we go again," said Jerry as he dumped an old coffee can full of crawdads back into the lake. "We're late for school! Mrs. Starry's gonna give us the dickens!"

"I know! Don't remind me!" exclaimed Jay as he picked up his books, fingers still coated with green threads of algae. "We've caught it from her before. It could be worse."

Up the hill they went, wiping their hands on their pants in little-boy fashion as they ran, stopping every now and then to retrieve a dropped book. Jerry opened the schoolhouse door and entered the entrance hall of the one-room school.

"I have to go potty," Jay blurted out in an attempt to avoid punishment as long as possible. Besides, Jerry got the brunt of Mrs. Starry's anger this way.

"Okay," Jerry volunteered. Jay was younger than Jerry and Jay always went potty before catching it at home too, so he wouldn't wet his pants and catch it worse for his lack of control.

"Where have you been since you're late for school? What were you doing that made you late and where is your brother?" Mrs. Starry managed to deliver all of this without taking a breath and it always left Jerry a little amazed as to how she managed to do it. And to think, he had just walked through the cloakroom and stepped into the classroom!

"Jay went to the john," mumbled Jerry as he surveyed his shoes and pants realizing for the first time how wet he was. The "john" was what the boys called their outdoor toilet that sat about 200 feet behind the schoolhouse and just beyond the swing set. The girl's toilet was called the girl's "john" by the boys.

"Take off your wet shoes and socks and come up by my desk," demanded Mrs. Starry.

Jerry walked slump-shouldered into the cloakroom hardly noticing the exclamation marks made by jackets hanging on hooks with boots at their base. The over-clothes seemed to come to life in the dim light afforded by two windows high up on the west wall and on either side of the door to the entranceway and outside.

Jerry tried to stay against the windowed wall, looking back as his mind saw some of the jacket arms reach for him. "I saw them move," he whispered to himself as he continued to walk towards his wall hook that had no jacket or boots waiting for him. He placed his shoes, toes toward the wall, and his cap he placed upside down, bill straight down and toward the wall, and laid his wet socks across his shoes. Slowly, in his same slump-shouldered way, he made his way back into the classroom.

Jay heard Mrs. Starry's scolding voice as he walked past the partially opened window and slowly entered the entrance hall. As he entered the cloakroom, he instinctively glanced toward his empty wall hook next to his brother's hook and noticed how Jerry's wet shoes and socks were placed neatly on the floor. Jay also noticed his wet feet and hurriedly removed his shoes and socks placing them directly under his wall hook, not seeing the symbolism of Jerry's clothes hanging in nonconformity with the other student's clothes.

"Get in here!" shouted Mrs. Starry as she opened the cloakroom door and surprised a daydreaming Jay.

Wow! thought Jay as he picked himself up off the floor in a daze. *How come I didn't hear her?* Little did he realize that he spent most of his young life with his imagination running way out ahead of himself. Mrs. Starry knew Jay's delay was halfway planned so he'd miss out on her initial anger. She also knew that he may well wet himself if his anxiety rose too high. She smiled slightly to herself as she reflected on how Jay's thought process was revealed in his actions. Of course, Mrs. Starry didn't realize that her inward smile lit up her face just enough for a small boy slightly spoiled by the older females in his family to notice. It betrayed the stern tone of her voice.

"Good morning, Mrs. Starry," Jay said with a smile warm enough to melt the hardest of hearts. "I'm just putting my wet shoes and socks in the cloakroom."

As Jay looked down at his bare feet, he noticed his wet pants for the first time. Jay decided that he'd better hurry to avoid further anger, so he went quickly into the classroom.

"Stand up by my desk," Mrs. Starry said as she surveyed her classroom for any misbehavior. The misbehavior stopped momentarily until the teacher turned away from the other students. As Jay walked confidently up to the only desk at the front of the classroom, he could feel more than fifteen pairs of eyes resting on him. Older boys and girls were talking in the background and snickering in anticipation of someone besides themselves getting punished. As Jay turned to stand by the desk, he noticed his older brother standing in the corner facing the wall and vaguely resembling his clothes in the cloakroom.

Golly, thought Jay, *no wonder everyone is snickering at me! At least there is no other free corner for me to stand in!*

"Jay! I want you to write on the blackboard one hundred times, I will not be late for school anymore!" Mrs. Starry ordered.

"Gosh, Mrs. Starry, I don't know how many one hundred are," fibbed Jay as he hoped to get out of his punishment.

"Just number each sentence up to ten and do those ten times and you'll have done it one hundred times," Mrs. Starry told Jay.

"Oh, no!" muttered Jay under his breath as he realized that now he had to do more than just write one hundred sentences.

I know, thought Jerry, thinking he got the worst punishment, *teacher sure likes Jay more than she likes me.*

Jay started writing on the blackboard, happy to get out of his studies for a while. "Jay! Do that at recess time and after school. Get to your studies now!" Mrs. Starry said, realizing that she had to stay a step ahead of Jay or he got his way inadvertently.

Jay made his way back to his desk thinking to himself, *Teacher likes Jerry more, obviously, since Jerry got punished less severely.* Neither boy realized that they both thought they were punished more severely only because Mrs. Starry knew just what punishment was best for each!

Jay got to work in preparation for reading class. He always had to learn his lesson completely since he was the only student in his grade. The reading class was Jay's first class in the morning and he hadn't finished all of his required work, so, he was a bit nervous. Classes were held up in front of the schoolroom at one of the two tables in the room. The teacher sat at one side of the table and students at the other side of the table. Any student not at the table could listen in if they wanted.

The first graders, two of them, went to the table at Mrs. Starry's request and so the actual schooling began. (Jay realized that he and his brother had missed the daily Pledge of Allegiance made to the flag.) Picture books were opened and pictures of items, the first letter of which matched the first letter of the items pictured, i.e., the letter *C* had a cat by it, and so on. Letters and their corresponding pictures were located, matched, and the letters recited. As Jay heard "*A* is for apple," he forgot what he was supposed to be doing and his mind went to the house-orchard across the road. *Wow!* thought Jay. *Last week at recess I saw the biggest and greenest apples a tree ever had!*

In the background Jay's mind caught. "*B* is for boy." *And boy,* thought Jay, *that green ole apple I ate last week gave me the meanest ole bellyache—even big enough for a man!* Again, his mind caught "*C* is for cat." *That ole cat of Miss Mary's next door liked to scare me outta that tree when I grabbed its tail for a branch to pull myself up.*

"*D* is for dog" came into his head as Jay's book fell from his hand with a clatter to the floor and his glassy eyes stared off into the distance and just happened to connect with the same kind of stare from the teacher, except her stare was for a different reason.

"Wee," said Jay as he glided through the air after his dog. Jay stopped in his dream with a thump on the ground and found himself instead, sitting alone at one side of the table in front of the room with not a brown-eyed dog face looking at him but instead an obviously upset Mrs. Starry face, eyes unblinkingly staring into his eyes.

"Aah," yelled Jay as he jumped off his chair sideways and fell sprawling to the floor. "Where am I and where did my dog go?" he asked as he picked himself up, walked back to his desk, and realized the roar of the wind he thought he heard was laughter coming from everyone else in the schoolroom.

"Get your reader and come up here!" ordered the teacher. "Students, be quiet!" she demanded as she turned and looked toward the back of the room.

Oh, no! Jay yelled to himself. *A whole number has gone by on the clock and I haven't read my lesson.* Jay had to learn as he read it for the first time all the while trying to ignore the snickers of older and younger girls and boys. Mrs. Starry made Jay answer every question at the end of the chapter.

"Now, Jay," she said, "if you had read your lesson as you were told, I wouldn't need to punish you. So tomorrow you may stay in at recess and write on the blackboard fifty times 'I will learn my lesson as I am told and I will not daydream in school.' The earlier punishment still stands too," she said.

Oh no! thought Jay. *They'll have to get more blackboards just on account of me!*

Since Jay's lack of study had caused Mrs. Starry to take more time than was allowed for Jay's reading class, she did a fast review and assigned the following day's work more hurriedly than usual.

Reading and math classes came and went for all grades without a problem. Recess came. When all of the students were excused to go outside to play, Jay was nabbed by Mrs. Starry and redirected to the front of the schoolroom by the blackboard.

"Gosh, Mrs. Starry, I forgot about writing on the blackboard," Jay blurted in his own defense while he hoped his "mistake" would not add to his already-hefty load of punishment.

"Don't worry, Jay," countered Mrs. Starry. "Part of my work here is to keep you heading in the right direction." Keeping Jay heading in the right direction is precisely what Teacher did too, much to Jay's dismay.

"Before you begin, Jay, please wash off the front blackboard and dust the erasers," requested Mrs. Starry. Mrs. Starry knew Jay and she knew that he would just give her more little boy nervous trouble if he were to miss a bit of fresh air at morning break.

"Yes, Mrs. Starry," answered Jay as he went outside to get water for washing.

He took the erasers with him to save him from having to face the teacher again, not because he was efficient. Jay dusted off the erasers on the sidewalk as other students had done in the past. *Wow!* thought Jay as he dusted the heavy felt erasers. "Whoever was supposed to do this last afternoon did a poor job!" he said out loud to himself as he remembered that it was his duty yesterday. Chalk dust got smeared all over his hands, face, and clothes as he kept pounding the erasers on the concrete sidewalk making his time outside last as long as possible. Jay picked up the empty red and white enamelware tub with the rag in it and went over to the water pump. The tub and rag were put down under the pump spout to catch the water.

As Jay pumped the handle up and down, out came the water with a splash as it hit the bottom of the empty tub. It splashed all over the ground and Jay as it came out in spurts as Jay continued to work the hand pump. *Boy,* thought Jay as he kept pumping the handle, *that looks just like me when I had the stomach flu! Ma said I couldn't keep a thing down.*

Jay went back into the classroom, washed the blackboard, and began his punishment realizing that he dared not push Mrs. Starry any further this morning. He got ten sentences of his first "blackboard" work finished during the rest of recess.

"Jay!" called Mrs. Starry. "Please ring the school bell for me so the other students know that recess time is over."

"Yes, Mrs. Starry, I will," replied Jay as he placed his chalk on the blackboard tray, hurriedly left the front of the room and made his way to the cloakroom. The rope connected to the bell hung down just out of Jay's reach. This was done on purpose to keep the smaller children from ringing the bell at inopportune times. Jay spotted a small chair and quickly slid it under the rope. Up he climbed. He was able to grasp the rope when he stood on his tiptoes. There was a big knot on the bottom end of the rope to keep the bellringer's hands from slipping off the rope as the bell was rung. The bell was quite heavy so the rope was put over a large pulley up by the bell to allow a mechanical advantage to the person ringing the bell. Jay grabbed the rope in both hands and pulled down with all of his might.

He found himself hanging in the air as he needed all of his weight to ring the bell. The bell slowly rolled backward as Jay pulled down with all of his weight. The bell emitted a weak *ding* as it tipped back slowly on its pivot point. The rope came down with the bell as the bell's motion returned beyond its starting point and landed Jay back on the chair with a bit of slack in the rope. The bell traveled faster after changing direction as gravity and Jay's weight pulled it "downhill" again on its pivot point. The slack in the rope tightened up and lifted Jay into the air since the bell traveled a bit farther in its forward motion. A deep-toned *DONG* sounded out and Jay began to come down with the bell rope, his weight helping to accelerate the bell in its downward journey.

"Wee!" squealed Jay as he descended about eighteen inches. A loud clear-toned *DING* sounded out this time as the bell traveled at a faster rate. Jay grinned like a kid on a carnival ride as this process was repeated several times with the bell seemingly wagging on its pivot point.

"Jay! Get down from that chair. The other students have been warned enough that recess is over," said Mrs. Starry.

Jay let go of the rope and let the bell come to a rest in its own good time. The bell ringing mechanism broke last year because of older boys riding on the rope. A neighbor man had fixed the bell—"so it will never break again" were his words.

On his way back to his desk, Jay noticed that he had filled one of the four blackboards that stretched across the front of the classroom with ten of his punishment sentences. At lunch time he would fill at least two, he promised himself as he opened his English book and began studying. English class came and went without incident, even though it lasted longer than any other class. Jerry finished his punishment just before lunchtime; however, he was allowed to attend his classes.

Lunchtime came. Two students had prepared the hand-washing line ahead of time by heating up a teakettle of water on an electric hot pad to be just more than lukewarm. They put hand soap at the front of the line where the warm water was, and they completed the hand washing line by getting a brown roll of paper towels for drying hands. One student poured a small amount of warm water on the first person's hands and they stepped aside to the soap. The next one got warm water on their hands as the first used soap. The first one then placed their hands back over the basin to get the soap rinsed off as the second one used the soap. The first one advanced to the next student holding the heavy brown roll of paper towels, and this process continued until all pairs of hands were cleaned. Lunches were cold and usually packed by moms who got up early in the morning, made the family breakfast, and then packed lunches for the children still attending grade school. Many students checked out each other's lunches, trading for what they could from each other's lunches to "better" their lunch in their own minds.

After eating, Jay had to be reminded again to continue his punishment. "Sorry. I forgot, Mrs. Starry. It's a good thing that I have you to remind me," Jay blurted as he took his place at the blackboard.

Mrs. Starry had to turn her head to hide her laughter so she didn't betray her emotions to Jay. She had to remind herself that these were some of the moments that made teaching worthwhile.

The other children played softball at noon recess. They made just enough noise to filter in to Jay writing at the blackboard. Jay heard the occasional "you're out" and "home run" and batter up." He fought hard as he continued to write *I will not be late for school; I will not be late for school; I will not be*—but it was just no use.

I will not be…struck out by a pitcher like you, came into his head as he stood at the blackboard. *CRACK!* went a bat outside on the ball diamond as Jay saw himself at bat in his mind. Away he went running bases as he stood in place holding a piece of chalk. (If someone could have seen him and gotten into his mind at the same time they would have laughed at the contradiction his inactivity at the blackboard made against his overactive mind.) Around the bases, wide around second and across third base he went running as he looked over his shoulder to try and see how far he had hit the ball. The ball came across the field like a horizontal shot as he slid across home plate and was pronounced "safe." The hero of the game, no less! Everyone clapped him on the back in gratitude since he had cleared the bases of runners. Even though his home-run excitement was dying down, he was still being clapped on the shoulder.

"Jay!" said Mrs. Starry as she tried to break him from his daydream by tapping him on the back. "I think I need to have you write your punishment on paper at home so you may finish your punishment and get on with your class studies at school. I will give a note to your sister to give to your mother so that she may help you complete your punishment. Parents backed up the teachers and followed through on punishments meted out because they knew it was for the benefit of their children.

Mrs. Starry realized that little boys like Jay needed no help in misbehaving and that is why she would give the note to one of Jay's sisters. Looking at Jay still full of chalk dust, Mrs. Starry realized how real an old definition of a small boy was—"noise in dirty pants."

The second half of the day was always the slowest part. The students watched the clock more in anticipation of the school day's end in the afternoon. The key-wound regulator clock had been replaced just after the war with a large round black-cased electric clock because it was supposed to be more accurate. Of course, since the electricity was off almost as much as it was on, this clock, too, labored for accuracy.

Social studies, which included geography for the lower grades and world events or history for the upper grades, went well. However, Jay got nervous while waiting for the end of the school day. He raised his hand to be noticed so he could go to the toilet. There was a two-sided paper sign on the inside knob of the door. One side of the sign had a green "GO" on it. The other side had a red "STOP" on it. The green "GO" meant that no one else was outside and at the toilet. The red "STOP" meant that someone else was at the toilet. All a student had to do was to turn the sign over as he or she went through the door. This was so Mrs. Starry could tell at an instant if she had given someone else permission to leave the room and go outside to the toilet. Some of the students forgot as young people often do, that the teacher had a secondary way of knowing if someone were outside. By simply doing a visual check of the desks and seeing a student at each desk, Mrs. Starry could easily see if all students were present or not.

After Jay returned from the toilet, Joan put her hand up to seek permission to leave the schoolroom to go to the toilet. Since it was getting close to afternoon recess time,

Mrs. Starry did not usually honor such requests. However, she did allow Joan to leave. Joan and a girlfriend of hers had made a plan at lunchtime to somehow both go to the toilet just before recess time, thus extending their recess. The two girls had included another girlfriend in their plans. As Joan was going out the door, Mary had her hand up to presumably get help with her studies since Mary held a book up for Mrs. Starry to see. Mary was talking to Lynn who sat just ahead of Joan. Joan's friend Betty raised her hand to be allowed to go to the toilet. Mrs. Starry glanced perfunctorily around the room (remember, she was also teaching a class) and gave Betty her permission to leave.

Joan and Betty walked in the tannery on their extended recess to avoid being seen. The tannery had been out of use since shortly after the turn of the century, (between fifty and sixty years) but still kept its name even though no buildings remained nor did any activity go on there. Part of the tannery had been on a small wooded hill on a path up from the boy's john and was just past the pond. The tannery had beautiful maple and other hardwood trees plus green carpets of soft, shaggy, flowing grasses that beckoned to many students on warm autumn and spring afternoons. The girls had fun talking as they walked with no one to distract them.

Mrs. Starry dismissed the class she was teaching and told all of the students to get ready for recess. She stood in front of the classroom with a pleased smile on her face as all of the students stood up and rushed towards the door as they were excused for recess. Joan and Betty noticed the others being let out and hurried back to the school grounds. Mary met the two and told them that Mrs. Starry must not have noticed them 'cause she said nothing and asked no questions about them. The two girls were pleased because they were wondering if their extended recess had been worth the deception put over on the teacher.

Jay had to stay in for recess time to study his science before class time. Remember, he was the only student in second grade and had to answer all the questions and do all of the reciting that would be required for the class.

Mrs. Starry went to the bell rope and rang the bell for the end of recess. Students came slowly in from play. Joan, Betty, and Mary came in together smiling happily. They felt a bit of relief when they went past Mrs. Starry with no rebuke from her.

The first graders were called up front for class. They had paperback books resembling coloring books in size. Their class consisted of general information about clouds and water and the cycle of water to rain. They had been required to color the clouds and sky according to how they thought it would look as the weather indicated, i.e., they had to color clouds stormy-looking if rain were indicated in their books and just white and fluffy-looking if the sun was shining and the sky was a deep blue.

Jay was called up next for science class. He was at a point in his book that paralleled the first graders' studies. He was learning about the different cloud types and how they were formed. Lightning was also a topic at this point. Jay had learned his subject well and teacher told him so. *He is such a mixed little personality*, thought Mrs. Starry as she listened intently to his answers to questions that were listed at the end of the chapter.

"Have you looked at the next chapter?" asked Mrs. Starry.

"Yes, I have, Mrs. Starry," said Jay. This chapter dealt with weather's effects upon plants, animals, and humans. This chapter was discussed too. Tomorrow's assignment was given before classes were dismissed.

Science classes came and went. Next, came spelling. Spelling class and art class rotated. One day spelling was the last class of the day and the next day art was the last class of the day. Spelling class was conducted with all students paying attention to all of the spelling lessons. The class took place with students staying at their desks too. Mrs. Starry was a firm believer that all would benefit from hearing all the words, their spelling, and their meanings recited to them. Some days, when all students had their studies done correctly and time remained, Teacher read an ongoing book to the class. The current book being read was *Tom Sawyer* by Mark Twain. Jerry and Jay felt a kinship with Tom and Huck even though they had a river and Jerry and Jay just had a lake to experience.

The end of the day was at hand. Jay had made it through without too much trouble. Mrs. Starry stood up in front of the class and went through the dismissal ritual. Just before she was ready to dismiss everyone, she said, "Joan, Betty, and Mary," as she winked at Jay sitting in the front row. "You three owe me morning recess tomorrow for your extended recess this afternoon. You may also owe me more because you took advantage of me while I was busy. I am responsible for your well-being while you are here. I will think it over this evening and let you know in the morning."

Jay smiled back at Mrs. Starry. He, like other students, was not particularly happy that others were getting punished. He was only happy that he was not being punished. He also knew that this was a worse form of punishment having to worry overnight about what would be dealt out tomorrow. He knew Mrs. Starry well and the wink told him that nothing bad would happen tomorrow, but he also knew that he would not tell this to Joan, Betty or Mary as Mrs. Starry also knew he would not tell this to them.

Jay's older sister had been given his punishment slip to give to his parents. He knew his night would be spent writing, but it would clear the slate and tomorrow would be a new day!

After the bus dropped Jay and his siblings off, he had a request for his older sister, "Sherry, will you please give me time to tell Mom and Dad about my trouble for today?"

"I will under one condition, Jay."

"What's a condition?" asked Jay, sporting a confused look.

"A condition is something that you have to do before your request is honored," answered Sherry as she smiled down at Jay.

"What is the con, con…dition you have in mind, sis?" asked Jay, suddenly more serious than before. He wondered what he would have to do now to avoid catching the dickens more at home.

"The condition, Jay, is that you need to tell Mom and Dad before we eat super tonight."

"Okay, sis, but can you help me a bit?" asked a crest-fallen Jay.

"Okay. What do you need help with this evening?"

"I need more time to tell 'em what happened. Please make supper later so Dad can rest before I tell 'em so he won't get more mad at me."

"Jay, Dad gets angry with you," said his sister as she tried to help him with his grammar.

"So, you noticed it too?" asked Jay in an innocent way as he studied his sister's face for signs of understanding.

"That is not what I meant for you to understand, Jay," said Sherry with a chuckle.

"Well, what did you mean?"

"First off, Dad does not get any angrier with you than he does with the rest of us, Jay. It only seems so because you may not be paying attention when the rest of us upset Dad. Do you understand that?"

"Okay, if you haven't noticed that he does."

"What haven't I noticed that Dad does, Jay?" asked Sherry as she sported a confused look on her face.

"If you haven't noticed that he gets angry with me more'n he does with you, Sherry," explained Jay.

"Anyway, Jay, I was correcting your speech." (She was going to say "people get angry with you") but she thought she would confuse him more so she said this instead: "People don't get 'mad' at another person, Jay. They get angry with another person. Mrs. Starry says dogs get mad; people get angry."

"Okay. I understand, but I forgot what I asked you before you told me about Dad not getting mad, I mean angry at…er with me. Did I say it right?" asked a learning Jay.

"You said it correctly, Jay," answered a very pleased older sister thinking Jay understood exactly what she said and that he understood it all on the same learning level as she understood. "You asked me if I would help delay supper a bit so Dad has a chance to rest from work so he may be more relaxed before you tell him about the trouble you got into today."

"Did I say all of that?" asked Jay with a doubting look on his face.

"You said it, but not exactly as I said it," added Sherry.

"So can you?" asked Jay for the second time in his mind.

"May I, Jay is—"

"Will you help me?" interrupted a bewildered Jay.

"Jay. I will help you as much as I can. I don't want to delay supper too long, though. I don't want Dad to be upset with me either," Sherry managed to say to her little brother.

"Okay. Thank you," said a still-confused Jay as he thought he better leave well enough alone to avoid asking for another explanation. He also wondered why some people had to say something using up all those words when just a few words would be enough. *Besides,* he continued to think, *there might not be enough words left over for the rest of us.* He also noticed that his brother and other sister had finished their meager chores and left the house until suppertime.

"Jay?" said his brother, Jerry, as he went running past Jay still standing where he stood when he first got off the bus.

"What do you want, Jerry?" asked Jay with a questioning look on his face.

"Hurry up and get your clothes changed so we can do something together before suppertime," stated Jerry.

"All right," said Jay as he looked down at himself still standing where he had been when he first got off the bus. *I must a been standing here a long time,* thought Jay to himself as he slowly walked toward the house.

"Where have you been, Jay?" asked his mother. (Jay picked up his pace as he heard Mom calling out to him.) "I have been calling for you. It is your turn to help get the table ready for supper tonight." Every night it was one of the boys' turn to remove the dining room chairs from the wall they rested against all day and put them around the table.

"I forgot," said Jay as he hurried upstairs and began taking off his clothes, laying them on the bed he and his brother slept in. "I'll change my clothes first, Mom," said Jay toward the stairs so his mother would hear him.

"Okay. Just hurry it up. We don't want to delay supper and upset your father tonight. He has a town meeting to attend after supper. The town meetings make him angry enough without our helping."

"Oh, Mom," said Jay as he began to understand how his early evening was going.

"Why, Jay, whatever is the matter?" asked Mother in a concerned voice as she made her way to the bottom of the stairs so Jay would hear her speak.

"Well," said Jay hesitantly.

"Well, what?" asked Mother back.

"Well, Mom, I kinda got into a bit of trouble today at school," fessed up Jay in a sheepish voice as he started down the stairs so he could help in the dining room.

"Oh! Jay! What kind of trouble?" asked Mother.

"Well, Jerry and I got to school late so we—"

"What do you mean that Jerry and you got to school late?" returned Mother as her eyes widened with each word she spoke.

Wow, thought Jay to himself, *those eyes are coming outta Mom's head soon if she keeps talking.*

"Well, Mom, we were early when we left home this morning, so I don't exactly know what happened."

"Jay, you and your brother walked to school this nice spring morning," reminded Mother as she stood still waiting for the story to be told.

"Yes. We did walk this morning. We had some fun along the way too."

Jay's mind wandered quickly back to the morning's walk to school.

He was currently by the lake in his mind recalling events of the morning.

"Jerry!" exclaimed Jay. "Look at the big crawdads on this big piece of bog." In some places the grass grew on bogs of mud and roots that were attached to shore on their close edge but floated on the edge by the water.

"What do you want, Jay?" said an excited Jerry.

"I want you to see the big crawdads on the underside of this bog," said Jay as he grabbed the big piece of bog by the grass much as one would grab a person by their hair. Jay pulled the bog up toward himself, exposing all of the aquatic life that clung to the underside of the bog. A huge crawdad about eight inches long tried to flip itself into the water but a quicker Jay grabbed

him just behind his great pinchers. "Look at him, Jerry!" shouted Jay. "He's as big as the one you caught yesterday morning, maybe bigger!"

"No way Jay!" challenged Jerry as he made his way to his brother.

"Jay. Jay. JAY!" yelled a mother whose patience just plain ran out.

"Who's talking?" asked a slightly confused Jay.

"I'm talking," supplied his mother. "I suppose you both got wet playing in the lake too." Mother made the accusation just to see if Jay were paying attention. And he was paying as much attention as a small boy may pay. (The payments were made slowly over a long period of time. There was no interest, and dividends equaled the interest in this case.)

"Yah, we did, Ma. Maybe that made us late."

"Didn't you walk with other students this morning?" asked Mother.

"We did, Mom. But they must 'a went a different way 'cause we were alone most of the way there," said Jay through squinting eyes as he tried to remember way back to the morning.

"Anyway, Jay, what else did you two do?" asked Mother as she just assumed that he and his brother got wet playing in the lake and that they both never realized that they did so quite often.

"Well, Jerry was okay the rest of the day," answered Jay, thinking but mostly hoping he had said enough.

"Jay, tell me the truth!" exclaimed Mother in a slightly raised voice as she unconsciously began to slowly tap her right foot on the floor. Jay had gotten dressed and had gone down the stairs to speak directly to his mother. Now he stared down at her gently taping foot, not knowing if he dared to speak or not. One would guess that he would not have a future in diplomacy if they only heard him as he spoke about so small a thing and made it sound so big because of his unhidden attempt at avoiding more punishment. Punishment and small boys mix like oil and water, and the boys always seem to get themselves in deeper the more they stall.

"Well, Mom," said a sullen Jay, "I might as well tell you the truth."

"Is there any other way to tell anything, son?" asked his mother.

"I kinda suppose not, Mom. I caught the dickens from Mrs. Starry 'cause I guess I was not con…concentrating on what I was doing or something," stammered Jay as he got as close to the truth as he dared and still claim to be a small boy.

"Did you have to write something on the blackboard as a punishment?"

"How did you know?" asked Jay with a wide-eyed look on his face.

"Mothers are supposed to know what their children don't actually tell them, Jay. Didn't you know that?"

"Really," said Jay not quite under his breath. His mother smiled as she saw belief written on his face. "I had to write that 'I will not be late for school anymore' Mom," finished Jay or so he thought.

"Is there anything else you want to unburden yourself with, Jay?" asked Mom as she decided she better get back to making supper happen or she would be the one to disappoint Dad.

"There might be," said Jay as he tried to think of a good way to tell on himself. Telling on oneself is a good way to turn the table around. It also builds character as it tears down the self-image. "I also had to write that 'I would learn my lessons and I wouldn't daydream anymore' too," said Jay as he finished telling on himself.

"Did you get all of this done in school today?" asked Mother in a credulous voice.

"No, Mom, I didn't," said Jay. His older sister heard her cue and added to the conversation.

"Mrs. Starry gave me a note for you today, Mother," said Sherry as she worked to help get supper ready.

"She did," stated Mother. "And what did the note say?"

"The note said that Jay needs to write his sentences at home tonight and get them to Mrs. Starry in the morning because he was taking too much time to write them on the blackboard. She also said that he was halfway finished with the first sentences. She said he needed to get them all in on time before class time tomorrow." Like Mrs. Starry, she, too, said all of this without taking a breath thought Jay as he turned toward Mother to see what her reaction would be.

"Well, Jay, you better get your sentences started before suppertime. How many do you need to do yet? That's right. Sherry said you did half at school. That means you have fifty of the first sentences and fifty of the second sentences left to write."

How did she do that? asked Jay of himself.

"Oh, Jay. Don't bother your father with such things tonight; he already has enough to think about."

"Okay, Mom!" said Jay as his countenance lit up. He began to leave the dining room to begin his sentences at home.

"Wait a minute, young man!" exclaimed Mother as she grabbed him gently by his shirttail. "You have to finish one task before you begin another."

"Oh, I almost forgot," said Jay as an excuse for his short attention span. (It hardly resembles a "span" since it is so ephemeral.)

So, Jay got out of telling Dad what happened at school today. He also knew that his mother would tell his father. They had their own way of understanding each other and settling their children's daily troubles. When Dad could not be at home to discipline a wayward child, Mom automatically stepped in in his stead and followed through with the punishment she thought appropriate. They never discussed the punishment they were determining with that child within hearing distance of their punishment discussion either. Just a few nonchanging rules helped to make them better parents. Something had to be extremely strange to make them not follow through for a teacher too. The last thing they wanted to do as parents was to undermine a teacher's authority in her classroom.

The old car was heard in the driveway and soon their father was at the door. He came in through the screen and storm door as he began to talk. "Is supper ready? I have to attend the town meeting tonight." He looked around for the paper to read. "Did, Dad, er...I mean did Grandfather speak to you about his attendance at the meeting tonight?" asked Father. Father changed his title for his dad to "Grandfather" because Mother's eyebrows rose as he said "Dad." This helped him to realize that his father was "Grandfather" when any of the children were within hearing distance and if they were not around, his father was Dad.

"No, dear, he did not," replied Mother as she continued to get supper on the table. "Was he going to the meeting with you tonight?"

"I thought he was. Maybe I need to run over there for a few minutes." Off went their father next door to see his dad.

"Why is Father going over to see Grandpa now?" asked Sherry.

"He went to make sure Grandfather is remembering about the meeting, Sherry," explained Mother as she finally got supper on the table.

"Dad," said his youngest son just as he popped his head through the kitchen door.

"My goodness, son!" exclaimed Grandmother. "You nearly startled me to death!"

"I'm sorry, Ma. I just wondered if Dad was going to the meeting tonight, that's all."

"Is that tonight?" asked Grandfather from the living room.

"Yes, Dad. It is."

"Well, I guess I better get ready for it, then. I don't want to be the only one not going. Besides it may well be interesting if our neighbor up the hill attends again tonight."

"I suppose he will. He usually attends."

"This'll be better than TV if he does," said Grandfather as he brushed past his son on the way to his bedroom to change clothes.

"I'll see you in half an hour, Dad. I need to have supper before the meeting. Lord knows it can be mighty irksome on an empty stomach."

"Dad is back!" announced Sherry as she came in from calling her siblings in for supper.

"I thought supper would be almost over for the rest of you since I took so long at Mom and Dad's."

"No, dear! We are running a bit late tonight. Just sit down and I'll finish up so we may all eat together as a family," finished Mom as she made sure all of the children were ready and in their proper places for dinner.

"Jay had a different day at school, Dad," said Jerry as he smiled widely at a scowling-faced Jay.

"I do not have time to pay attention tonight, I'm sorry Jerry," explained Dad as he ate in an unusually fast manner hardly tasting his food. "I need to finish eating so I will not be late tonight."

"Don't worry, dear," said Mother as she shushed Jerry much to the enjoyment of Jay. "I'll take care of the children's troubles." And she did.

Supper ended without much trouble. Mother made sure Jay got to work on his sentences so Mrs. Starry would know that she was supported at Jay's home. Jay worked well when he worked alone. He soon finished his punishment and was told to get to tomorrow's studies just as his brother and sisters were. If the children played before supper, they missed out on playing with the neighborhood children whose mother had them study first and play later. Just as the children were finishing up with their take-home schoolwork, their mother called up the stairs for them to finish and get ready for bed. This was an easy but time-consuming event most nights.

So, Jay and the rest of the family got ready for bed. Jay remembered to put his finished sentences inside the top book on his stack of homework books. Jay had a puzzled look on his face as he wondered why he had homework. *What use is it anyway?* wondered a yawning Jay, suddenly a tired Jay. *I'll ask Mom in the morning,* he answered himself as he fell down into bed asleep as his head hit his cotton batting pillow.

Mom usually had the rest of the children brush their teeth after Jay so they helped push him to get ready for bed. It usually worked. Jay dreamed as young boys do and consequently made much noise and thrashing about in the night. His older brother was often deprived of a full night's sleep for this reason.

The morning came quickly. Dad was always long gone to work before anyone else got up…well, except for Mom. She always got up and made breakfast for Dad, usually just coffee. They probably did their best talking in the morning. I do not know for sure 'cause I was never there to listen. Dad also read in the morning.

"Jay!" said Jerry as he rolled sideways out of his bed. "Jay!" said Jerry a bit louder. "JAY!" said Jerry finally in his last attempt to get Jay out of bed and on his way to school.

"What do you want, Jerry?" asked a sleep-quenched Jay.

"It's time to get up for school, Jay," answered Jerry doubtfully as he watched Jay slowly slide back into the bed and close his eyes.

"Jay! Mom told me to get you up to get ready for school and you hafta get outta bed now."

"Okay, Jerry," said an almost-awake Jay. "I gotta make sure I get my home sentences in to school today," said Jay out loud to a bewildered Jerry.

"What do you hafta get to school, Jay?" asked Jerry.

"I hafta get my sentences in," replied a Jay already wrapped up in his own thoughts.

"I don't understand just what he's talking about," muttered Jerry softly to himself as he passed Jay and went down to breakfast just as Mother announced that it was breakfast time.

"Be right down!" answered Liddy.

And so another day began for the children. Mother had breakfast ready and school lunches prepared and packed away in lunch boxes. All of the children were ready and waiting as the bus turned into the yard and pulled up close to the house. It was a four-door sedan but it held six children and the driver. No seat belts in cars made for more seating. The school was only a mile away so sometimes they rode the bus and sometimes they walked. Their older sister informed the bus driver when the boys walked. This was a community in which most people were either related or close friends.

Mother had breakfast ready for all who wanted to eat and made sure each child took their lunch box with them. If you couldn't always eat breakfast, you at least had a lunch. That was her attitude about it. Jerry and Liddy were the first to be out waiting for the bus. Sherry and Jay followed soon after.

"Jay?" asked Sherry as she walked out with Jay to wait for the bus.

"Yes, Sherry?" answered Jay.

"Do you have your punishment sentences with you this morning so Mrs. Starry gets them right away today?"

"Yes, I do, Sherry. See these," said Jay as he showed his finished work to his oldest sister.

"Very good, Jay!" exclaimed Sherry as she glanced at the papers Jay showed her.

Jay got into the back seat of the bus as Sherry got into the front seat.

"Ouch!" shouted Jay as he moved away from the door to make room for his brother.

"I get the door side of the car, Jay!" pronounced Jerry with his head tilted back just a bit for emphasis.

"I don't care today," said a quiet Jay as he checked his book and made sure his sentences were still in his book. He was just happy to be done with yesterday's punishment.

Other children were playing catch-up on the ball diamond already as this, the last bus load of children was let off at the front of the school building.

"Hurry up and join us!" was shouted at the bus by several students as the bus arrived. So, the freshly arriving students hurriedly ran into the schoolhouse and dropped off their books and other papers, hollering back to those playing ball to be sure and keep a place for them as they readied to play ball.

Mrs. Starry rang the school bell finally indicating that it was time to stop playing and time to enter the schoolhouse in an orderly fashion. (Jay went to the boy's outhouse before entering the schoolhouse.) This being accomplished by all students, Mrs. Starry asked Jay to the front of the room and to her desk. "Jay. I need to see your completed sentences right away this morning so go to your desk and get them for me please."

"Okay, Mrs. Starry," replied a pleased and almost self-satisfied Jay as he made his way back to his desk. His top book had his papers in it. He opened his top-most book only to find it empty. A nearly panicked Jay raised his head to look towards the front of the classroom at Mrs. Story. She read the emotion on his face and went slowly to be by Jay at his desk.

"Well, Jay?" asked Mrs. Starry. "Where are your papers for me?"

"I don't know what happened, Mrs. Starry. I had them done and I put them in my book. They were still there when I went out to play before school started," continued a teary-eyed Jay as he frantically searched for his papers.

"Sherry?" called Mrs. Starry from Jay's desk.

Other students were looking towards Jay's desk trying to hear Mrs. Starry and Jay as the two discussed Jay's sentences. Sherry made it up to Jay's desk and asked, "What do you need of me, Mrs. Starry?"

"Just a minute, Sherry," pleaded Mrs. Starry as she turned to face the rest of the student body. "Students, please review your first morning class papers. I will be with you soon." She turned back to Sherry and said, "I need to know if Jay finished his sentences and bought them to school with him today," explained Mrs. Starry.

"I know he did them and that he had them with him on the bus this morning. I also saw them in his top book on his desk as he placed the books there before going out to play ball," finished Sherry.

"Very well, Sherry. Thank you. You may go back to your desk, but please check in the wastebasket at the back corner of the room on your way to your desk," requested Mrs. Starry quietly as she turned back to Jay. "Well, Jay what did you do incorrectly today?" she asked.

"I think I know this one, Mrs. Starry," said a sheepish Jay.

"What do you know?" asked Mrs. Starry as she looked up to see Sherry gently waving several papers in her left hand.

"I should have given my papers to you as soon as I came into the school today."

"Yes, Jay, you should have," said a very understanding Mrs. Starry. "I think everything will be fine in a few minutes," said Mrs. Starry as she turned and met Sherry as Sherry handed her several papers.

"How did you know where the papers would be, Mrs. Starry?" asked an incredulous Sherry.

"That basket gets emptied out only at the end of each day, Sherry," explained Mrs. Starry. "No one looks at it all day until the end of the day when it is dumped. Someone has taken Jay's papers and put them into the basket in hopes that he'll get into deep trouble with me right away this morning."

"That's terrible, Mrs. Starry!" exclaimed Sherry as she glanced at a bewildered Jay who quit looking for papers since he just realized that Sherry had located them.

"Who would want to get Jay into trouble!"

"I do not know right now, Sherry, but I will before the end of the day," assured a confident Mrs. Starry.

"Students!" demanded Teacher. There was a timed startled jump by all students as they turned their eyes to Mrs. Starry.

"Yes, Mrs. Starry?" asked the room full of students in unison.

"Students, I have a mystery to solve today," said Mrs. Starry with a confident look on her face.

"What kind of mystery?" asked several students.

"I'll leave that as a mystery at the moment!" answered Mrs. Starry as she hoped the "knowing" person or persons would give her a sign of guilt. She knew that there were a couple of children who would do such a thing just to postpone classes for a few minutes just to shorten the day a bit. She was also certain that the truth would reach the light of day. It usually did and did so faster if more than one child were involved. It just took so much more doing for more than one person to fool others. It would work for a while, but sooner-or-later the truth was revealed.

"First grade students!" demanded Mrs. Starry. "Come up to the class table please. The rest of you continue to complete what schoolwork you will." With that said, Mrs. Starry returned to her first graders and began the day's teaching.

So first graders got to tell Mrs. Starry once again, what they remembered from yesterday. She told them today's lesson since they had no formal textbook. They participated at the table in front of the rest of the students, as always.

"Jay," called Mrs. Starry as she prepared for second grade reading class. Jay had his reading assignment and book ready and went swiftly up to class. Mrs. Starry noticed two older students begin to talk and laugh as Jay made his way to the classroom table. She made a mental note of all of the movements and noises during the day's classes. "Have you finished your reading assignment and notebook work for today?" asked Mrs. Starry.

"Yes, Mrs. Starry. I am ready for class," answered Jay. So, reading classes met and finished in a timely manner, which gave time for the next classroom subject.

"Students," said Mrs. Starry. "Clear your desks off and get ready for recess." All students acted in unison as they cleared their desks and made ready for recess time. "You may go." Away they went. Mrs. Starry watched each student as they left the room. She noticed two older students, a boy and a girl speak to Jay as he left the schoolhouse. *Those are the same two who whispered at Jay's classroom time and laughed to each other,* Mrs. Starry thought to herself. Mrs. Starry decided that she would need to use assumption based upon her observed actions and reactions as she attempted to solve the day's mystery. She would eventually speak to those two students and hope for an honest answer in return.

Mrs. Starry rang the bell signifying the end of recess, as she did so, she noticed that the two students who were very interested in Jay and his troubles walked past her and then began talking softly about Jay's troubles with a bit of humor in their voices.

"Jay," said Mrs. Starry as Jay attempted to walk past her on his way into the classroom.

"Yes, Mrs. Starry?" asked Jay as he stopped to see what the teacher wanted of him.

"Jay, what did the two students ask you as you left for recess time a bit ago?"

"Well, Mrs. Starry, they said it was a shame that someone did such a thing to me to try to get me into trouble right away in the morning."

"Jay, did anyone else talk to you about your homework during recess?"

"No, Mrs. Starry. No one else talked to me about it," finished Jay as Mrs. Starry motioned him to return to his desk in the classroom.

Late morning classes went by with no difficulty as did afternoon classes after lunchtime. At the end of the day, Mrs. Starry was just about to dismiss students to go home, but before doing this, she went to the two students and asked them to stay after so she could talk to them.

"Students, you are dismissed. Don't forget your homework so you will be prepared for tomorrow's classes." All students got their books ready and left to take the bus home.

Two students waited nervously at Mrs. Starry's desk for her to return from releasing the others for going home. "What did you need us for?" asked the two students in near unison.

"I have several reasons to suspect you of sabotaging Jay with his sentence punishment," said Mrs. Starry. "Are you going to deny that it was you two who orchestrated the near destruction of Jay's punishment papers?" she asked.

"How did you guess that we were the ones who did it?" they asked.

"Well, I have my ways of knowing just as your mothers have their ways of knowing things about you that you don't come out and tell us. Let's just let it go at that; however, I'll need you both to write one hundred sentences that say 'I'll not interfere with Mrs. Starry's punishment assignments anymore.' Please hand them in first thing in the morning and hope that no one tries to dispose of your sentences the way you attempted to do to Jay's."

"Okay. Thank you, Mrs. Starry, good night," said the two students as they realized that they had gotten off lightly for the trouble they tried to get Jay into.

"Good night," replied Mrs. Starry as she realized that these two had not acted out of character for young students.

EASTER AFTERMATH

All of the students were happy! There would only be a half a day of school tomorrow, Good Friday. Classes would resume on the following Monday.

"Students!" called Mrs. Starry just before the last break of the Thursday before Easter weekend. "You all realize that tomorrow is Good Friday, don't you? You also realize that you will have the afternoon off tomorrow for religious services in case your family wants to attend church?"

All students nodded in affirmation as Mrs. Starry finished her announcements. All they could think about was that they would have a half a day off school this week! What a treat!

"What are you doing tomorrow afternoon?" said Ted to Jerry after they were released for recess.

"I suppose Mom will drag us to church somewhere," answered Jerry as he looked sideways at Jay hoping Jay wasn't paying attention. He was right. Jay was not paying attention. There would be no church for Jerry or Jay or any other people who stayed in the small settlement tomorrow since it was difficult enough to get a pastor to come for Sunday services and all but impossible for one to arrive for Good Friday services.

"Why? What are you doing tomorrow afternoon?" asked Jerry.

"We are going to town tomorrow," answered Ted. "Going to town" meant going to the county seat about twenty miles away. Most shopping for groceries and household goods was done there. Yes, there were churches there too. Ted's parents farmed, so they would be picking up the children from school and going directly to town to shop and get home in time for evening milking and other chores.

The recess break came and went with students dreaming of half a day of school tomorrow and what they would do with the seemingly endless hours they had just realized they would have for tomorrow and the weekend.

"I will see you tomorrow morning. We will be only having two classes tomorrow. I will read the Easter story to you the last hour of the morning," said Mrs. Starry. "This way those of you who cannot attend church services will be able to know what the day, Good Friday, means to many of us. When she had finished, she said, "So, get ready for recess now. When all of you are ready, you will all get to leave." Older students felt themselves aging as they waited for younger students to get ready for recess.

"Okay, you may all leave for recess now," Mrs. Starry said at last. When Mrs. Starry started saying "leave," the older boys were up and out the door.

It was a fine, early spring day and softball was on all of the boys' minds and some of the girls' minds. Workup was the game of the day every day! Everyone who had played last recess remembered where he or she finished before lunch ended. Smaller children played on the swing set or where they would. Too soon recess would end and the last leg of the day would begin.

The bell rang announcing that schooltime was next again. The last part of the day was a quick and easy part of the day. Many adults believed it was set up that way so students would not have to think too much with their minds divided about the day's end and class time.

The horn sounded outside, giving notice that the bus was ready for students. Quickly, Mrs. Starry got the day's fragments together and dismissed the students for the day reminding them of the half day of school tomorrow.

Friday started with a light, spring, misty rain. It was warm enough not to be sleeting. So school was not called off as some had hoped. There was a happy bustle in the school. Everyone was excited, anticipating the half day. It was so exciting! Since all students were in the school because of the rain, Mrs. Starry decided to ask if they would like to say where they would each spend the rest of the day. She said not to worry if it were not in a church to worship since she knew there would probably not be a minister available for the community, anyway. The older students talked first.

"Well, I think we are going to drive to Illinois this afternoon to visit relatives over the weekend," said Kelly almost sounding unsure and disappointed.

"We are going to 'town' this afternoon," said Ted. "Ma and Pa are picking Dale and me up here at school."

"We are all staying at home and will help Mother with any preparations needed," said Liddy "At least us girls will be helping, anyway," she finished as she shot an evil look at her brothers, Jerry and Jay.

"Yah," offered Jay suddenly since he had thought he would not have to speak. "Jerry and I have guy stuff to do." Guy stuff probably meant fishing by the lake. It was a good fun day that often yielded a good meal of fish at home.

Mrs. Starry asked if anyone else wanted to tell others of how they would spend the rest of the day, but no one else was forthcoming, so she read the Easter Story from a book of bible stories. When she had finished, she said, "Do any of you have questions about this story?" No one answered, so she assumed they all understood what she had read. Instead, each one was afraid to ask, thinking it would prolong the class time and delay the beginning of their Easter vacation.

"If there are no questions, then you may get ready for classes," said Mrs. Starry. Morning classes went well after which the children all scrambled to clear off their desks for classes. The hum of the bus's engine was heard outside as Mrs. Starry said, "You are dismissed for the weekend. Have a great Easter Vacation."

There was such a stampeding of tiny and not-so-tiny feet as you never before or since heard! Children "hurried" more in dismissal than at any other time or event. The bus made its way to children's homes in the usual manner as each child excitedly anticipated the gathering of friends and families for the Easter weekend.

Mrs. Starry had been correct in assuming that there would be no church services in the small community's church. There were no ministers willing to make the trip to the town for so few people who would be wanting to attend services.

Friday afternoon was a time for Jerry and Jay's mom and sisters to clean house in readiness for Sunday's company for dinner. Grandpa and Grandma, Mom's parents, would be coming to dinner as well as would be Dad's parents. Rarely were both sets of grandparents together with the family at the same time. It would be a fine day! Little thought was put on the religious aspects of the day. The girls did housecleaning as they were told. Jerry and Jay were caught by their mother as they tried to sneak out of the house.

"Boys," said Mother sharply as she went looking for them and saw them heading out the back door towards the lake. "Not so fast. We need you two to help with the cleaning by drawing water from the well. We will also have to wash clothes and hang them out to dry today since there will be baking to do tomorrow. We do not want to leave anything for Sunday but the final cooking of the meal."

So back into the house came a sulking Jerry and Jay. Such a perfect day for fishing and they had to help with housecleaning. They tried to wiggle their way out of chores, but it was no use! They took two pails, went to the well house, opened the water spigot, turned on the electric power to the pump and filled the pails with water for laundry and general housecleaning.

After the wash machine (this machine was a wringer-type) was filled with water, Jerry and Jay got the electric doughnut-style water heater, put the heating end down into the water in the washing machine and plugged it in to a wall electrical outlet. It would take about twenty minutes for water to get hot enough for clothes washing. "We better stick around, Jay," said Jerry. "If we don't, we will 'catch it' when Dad gets home, and besides, we need to help here."

"Okay, Jerry," answered Jay. "We'll stay! The fish will still be there."

The sisters finished their chores and the boys did as little as they could get away with as usual. Mother was always excited when company was expected. She bustled about straightening and cleaning until all looked ready to the children, but, then she found other work to do. There was much to do!

Easter finally arrived! Mom's folks had to travel about twenty miles while Dad's lived just next door and came early to chat and joke. Grandpa, Dad's father, was quite a storyteller.

"Did I tell you about the time I was a river rat on the Chippewa?" asked Grandpa, his eyes wide open and eyebrows raised as he looked at each of his grandchildren in turn.

"No, Grandpa!" sang all of the kids together. They probably heard the story many times but just wanted to hear it again. Grandpa never told the story quite the same way twice. His stories were true in the most part, but young children can't always tell that part from the other parts. One thing was always true and that was that his stories were always interesting.

"Well," said Granddad, "I was no more than nineteen when I was working on the Chippewa for a logging outfit. It had to be about '06. We worked hard back then. No power saws; at least the owner of the outfit never bought one for us to use. We used two-man saws, wedges, and a sledgehammer to drive the wedges into the cut we made opposite the notch an axe-man made just before we did our sawing. We felled many trees in a day. This was a big outfit with over a hundred men in it. We worked hard, so we drank hard." Grandpa had quit drinking in the late '40s. No fuss. He just quit.

"Is this a story the kids should be hearing, Granddad?" asked our mother as she was putting the finishing touches on the table while keeping an ear tuned to the story being told in the living room.

"Yes, I think it won't hurt them," said Grandpa as he continued with his story. "A couple of the guys decided to bring out their bottles of whiskey and pass them around. Our cook was known to have a fondness to such things as whiskey so some of the men thought that if they let him imbibe for a while, he might be persuaded to fix a late-night snack. So Cookie and about ten of us guys sat around drinking and talking until quite late, or, rather, early.

"'Say, Cookie,' said Bill. 'Do you think we could get a bite to eat tonight?'

"'Why I do believe so,' said Cookie as he left with a whiskey bottle and headed for his kitchen. He had two large raccoons hanging on the lines on the left side of his camp kitchen.

"He asked two of the men to skin the coon and bring them into his kitchen. All three of the guys had too much to drink, but soon Cookie was cooking a meal. He had no nose for game but he never spoiled a meal by over-seasoning. This was his redeeming quality! Soon the door on the kitchen opened and in Cookie came with a large platter of meat. It smelled good to men who worked at camp for up to a month at a time before seeing *their families and for a day of home cooking, and then coming right back to work.*

"'Come and eat!'" shouted Cookie to those still out of their bunks. And eat we did," said Grandfather as his eyes twinkled in fond memory. "We ate our fill. Never had raccoon tasted so good. We all went to bed full and ready to sleep, and we slept well in our bunks laid with marsh grass for mattresses. Our foreman was the second man up. Cookie was always first.

"'You better go out the side door and take a look, Cookie,' he said with a smile. Sure enough, Cookie went out one side door, looked and came back in the other side door with a white and sheepish look on his face. 'What's the matter?' the men asked.

"'Not much,' said Cookie. ''Cept that there's still two coon hanging on the left side of the kitchen and the two skunks on the right side are gone!' That was enough for most of the men. They turned green in the face. 'Just you wait a minute before you start complain'en! You all ate and slept well as far as I recollect!' It was true. We all did. You know," said Granddad. "I still don't know how skunk tastes!" He smiled so hard he almost laughed.

"Oh, Grandpa," said his grandchildren. "You don't expect us to believe that, do you?" There were footfalls on the porch floor that were heard by all. The kids jumped and ran to meet their other grandparents. Grandma was taller than Mom, but grandpa was taller yet. He was about five-foot ten and he weighed almost three-hundred pounds. He was ten years younger than Dad's dad and still worked for the railroad.

"Grandpa and Grandma!" sang the children as they mobbed their grandparents.

Grandma always had candy bars for the kids. Since Grandpa liked to drink a bit, she went along. Whenever someone bought a round of drinks, she would ask for a candy bar, which she put in her purse for later. Today was her later. Everyone greeted each other and Mother said, "It's time to eat. Please be seated. There is no particular order here, but Mom, please sit by me so we can chat while we eat. I won't have much time for chatting and it is so nice to see you."

"Well," said Grandma, "I suppose I could sit by you." And so she did. Mother had roasted a huge turkey that was stuffed, and had ham on the side. Potatoes, sweet potatoes, homemade rolls, and green beans rounded out the meal. There was always pie for dessert. It was a great dinner and both sets of grandparents gave the children all the attention they required. When dinner was over, Mom and her mother did the dishes and cleaned up the kitchen as they talked. The girls helped by bringing the dishes into the kitchen and scraping plates. Dad's mom had been a victim of polio when she was a little girl and she stayed close to a chair. Dad and his father-in-law smoked and talked away from the children. Grandpa and Grandma next door went home.

As the afternoon wore on, Mom's parents had to leave for home. It had been a nice day, but had moved swiftly by. School was looming on the horizon. Mom could tell because the kids were restless in the sureness of it.

"Sherry!" yelled Mother. "Get up. You'll miss the bus again!" Monday morning. Nothing ever changes. Down the stairs and out the door ran Sherry hoping to catch the bus.

"Wait!" she shouted. The bus came to a stop.

"I thought maybe you were staying home again," the bus driver said with a grin.

"Very funny!" shot Sherry back at him as she climbed in and sat nearest the door in back.

Back at school, softball was not the first thing on student's minds this morning. They all needed to talk about their weekends and the company they had for Easter dinner.

"Did you get to Illinois this past weekend, Kelly?" asked Sherry as soon as she saw Kelly while stepping off the bus.

"We had to stay home. Pa's help went away for the weekend and we had all he could do to keep up with the farm chores and other work," said Kelly.

"Didn't you and your brother help your dad?" asked Sherry.

"Yes. We did, but Dad decided to do extra cleaning since he gained a weekend. It almost ruined our weekend!" exclaimed Kelly.

The bell rang signaling the beginning of the school day. Mrs. Starry greeted the students at the entry door. "Good morning, students. Hello. How was your time off?

"How was my time off? It was great, thank you for your concern." Replied most students. Soon, all of the students were in the schoolhouse.

Attendance was taken and Mrs. Starry asked, "Who wants to lead in the Pledge of Allegiance this morning?" Again, many hands shot up. One student was picked. Somehow it always worked out so that no student got to begin the pledge two days in a row. Morning classes came and went with a relatively smooth transition.

It was lunchtime. Everyone could pretty well guess just what every other student had in his/her lunch box. Easter weekend always left an abundance of colored eggs to eat. Other students were already sitting down at their desks to eat as Jean went through the wash line, got her lunch pail, and sat at her desk. (The weather was still a bit too unsettled to eat outside.) As she looked through her lunch box she lit up with an idea. Small talk was heard as each lunch was being eaten.

"Mrs. Starry?" said Jean as if she had a question.

"Yes, Jean? What is it that you want?" answered Mrs. Starry as she got up from her desk and her lunch to go to see what Jean wanted. Slowly Mrs. Starry leaned over Jean's desk and put her head down to hear what Jean had to say.

A loud *whack* was heard by all in the room as Jean's hand was seen to swing through the air and land something solidly on the top of Mrs. Starry's head. Down slumped Mrs. Starry slightly in surprise as much as anything as a hard-boiled Easter egg cracked open on her head. The whole classroom was absolutely quiet as each student sat in shocked disbelief! Slowly the realization of what happened crept into each student's mind and a collective outburst of half-subdued laughter and pending doom filled the room.

Mrs. Starry rose up with her two hands clasping the body of Jean as she rose. "Whatever possessed you to think about doing what you did?" asked Mrs. Starry in pain and disbelief. "You should know better than to do that to anyone!" she yelled upset at the foolishness of one of her students and upset with herself too for falling into a not too well-thought out trap.

"We do this at home every year," said Jean in defense. "No one seems to mind."

"Well, you do not do it here!" said Mrs. Starry sternly. "You will stay in for recesses this week and after school today. You need to learn to have more respect for others than you obviously have now." With that, Mrs. Starry put Jean down in her desk chair, turned and went back to her desk and lunch. She realized that she, too, needed to show control in this situation. She also realized that at least half of the classroom of students saw humor in what just happened at her expense! She knew that recess time would allow the children to release the laughter still being held within. And, of course, she was correct!

The afternoon went by without unusual disruption. Jean had to stay behind at school and her mother showed up at school about a half hour after Jean should have been home. Jean was helping Mrs. Starry straighten up the books in the many bookcases around the room.

"Hello, Mrs. Starry," said Mrs. Aller.

"Hello, Mrs. Aller," said Mrs. Starry.

"Is everything okay? I was a bit worried when Jean didn't get off the bus today."

"We had an incident today at lunchtime, didn't we, Jean?" asked Mrs. Starry.

"Yes, we did, Mrs. Starry," said Jean.

"What are you talking about?" asked Mrs. Aller.

"Mom. I made a mistake at lunchtime today. I asked Mrs. Starry to come to my desk and when she did, as she bent down to ask what I needed, I hit her over the head with a hard-boiled egg. I know it was wrong, Mom, but—"

"You hit Mrs. Starry on the head with a hard-boiled egg?" asked Mrs. Aller in disbelief. "Is that true, Mrs. Starry?"

"Yes. It is true, Mrs. Aller," explained Mrs. Starry. "That is why I have Jean after school. She also will be in for recesses and lunch the rest of the week."

"She will get extra chores to do at home this week too!" said Mrs. Aller. "I can't believe you did such a thing! Are you okay, Mrs. Starry? Is your head fine?"

"Yes. I am okay."

"Mom, I told her I'm sorry. We do the egg thing at home all the time," said Jean in her own defense.

"I know we do it at home, Jean, but maybe we shouldn't anymore," said her mom.

"Thank you for being so very understanding about all of this, Mrs. Starry. Is Jean free to leave?"

"Yes, she is. I just wanted you to come and pick her up from school so we could talk. She has helped me to straighten the books on the library shelves since the end of classes," said Mrs. Starry. Jean and her mother left the school with everyone satisfied with the punishment meted out. Parents were concerned that their children showed proper behavior in all of their social dealings and usually sided with the teachers on issues that took place at school.

SPRING TROUBLE

It was a warm spring morning. The snow had all disappeared several weeks ago. The birds were all singing merrily in the trees. Truly a great time for two brothers!

"This is Friday, Jay," said Jerry as he pulled on his shoes. "We're free for two days after today," he added as he tied his shoelaces.

"You better get through today before you plan for tomorrow," advised Jay as he, too, pulled on and tied his shoes. "Friday is usually test day. Mrs. Starry always thinks she surprises us with an exam. You'd think by now that she would know that we're wise to her," finished Jay. Unbeknownst to Jay, Mrs. Starry pretended to surprise the students with a test every Friday. She knew they would at least learn for that reason alone, if they were not just aching to get the knowledge.

Jerry and Jay finished getting ready for school, ate their breakfast, and peeked into their lunch boxes.

"Mom made us a sandwich and put a piece of cake in with it," said Jerry while attempting to put on his spring jacket.

"I was still hungry after lunchtime yesterday, Mom," said Jay.

"You must be in a growth spurt again, son," said their Mom. "I'll pack another sandwich for each of you so you will be able to pay attention to Mrs. Starry all day through."

Jerry and Jay's two sisters were already outside waiting for the bus. The "bus" was a car that was driven by a neighbor. This car was driven to all of the children's homes to pick them up. He always had to make several trips to and from school. Sherry, the older sister, was many times late. She slept in for as long as possible almost every day.

"Sherry! Sherry!!" yelled the boys as the car/bus pulled into their driveway. The bus was really an early 1950s four-door sedan. It was fine for conveying boys and girls to and from school.

The front screen door on the house slammed shut just ahead of Mom's scolding voice, "Sherry! How many times have I told you not to slam the door! Now get a move on so you don't miss the bus as you did last week."

Sherry crossed the lawn and headed for the bus. Sherry was in sixth grade and physically mature for her age at eleven. She had blonde hair and was very easy to look at.

Most boys in eighth grade had noticed her and paid close attention to her whenever they could. She wasn't a ditz either. She was at the top of her class and all the students knew you had to "get up early" (but not too early, as we have seen) to outsmart her.

It was a Friday in May of the late 1950s. Sherry knew she was a bit late for the bus most days. She paid no attention to the taunting and teasing of other students when the others found out that she had been late, again. Sherry simply didn't care what they thought of her.

The school bell hammered out its usual *DING-DONG* to the students and the surrounding countryside. So, school began every day here as it had since the community first provided a school in the early 1890s.

"All of the students are tired looking and short-tempered today," whispered the teacher to herself as she saw some bickering back and forth. *They must have studied last evening,* was her self-said conclusion. "Good morning!" said Mrs. Starry as she resurveyed her students for attendance. She knew them all well and had no need to read off each name and listen for a "present" at the beginning of each day, but she did anyway just for the sake of order in the day.

"Children, we will stand with a hand over our heart and recite the Pledge of Allegiance. Who wants to start?" she added. All hands rose toward the ceiling as each tried to be the first to get their hand up. The first hand up was the one to begin saying the pledge to the flag and country. "Well, Jay, it appears that you had your hand up first this morning. You may lead us in the Pledge of Allegiance today," she finished.

Jay began the pledge and the other students followed: "I pledge allegiance to the flag of the United States of America and to the republic for which it stands, one nation, under God, indivisible, with liberty and justice for all!" Jay beamed with pride. It was an honor to lead in the morning pledge.

The first class was called to the table at the front of the classroom. The first-grade class, just Jay, was tested orally for ABCs and some words that had been learned. All went well. Second-grade was called up next. "Put your books away before you do anything else," Teacher commanded. Everyone knew what was coming next. They all dreaded it when their class time came, but they knew nothing would change the teacher's mind. The second-graders put their books away and got ready for testing. The teacher pulled no punches. She always had testing on Fridays and nothing changed it. No pleadings, no excuses, no tears.

The teacher was not hard. She simply led. She knew her place as a figure of authority and she used it justly. She was consistent and constant. If she had ever faltered, she knew she would lose control of the students. It only took one time and control was lost. She knew she was teaching more than just school subjects. She was also teaching one of life's lessons. The world did not change because you pleaded, gave excuses, or cried. She knew she was their teacher, not their friend. She taught that it was best to always be prepared. You never knew when your time was at hand!

Classes came and went. Recess and lunch came and went. Jerry and Jay waited for the last recess every day. Here they consumed their last bit of lunch. This helped tie them over until Dad came home at about five forty-five and Mom had supper ready by six in the evening.

Today Jerry and Jay were interrupted as they got their lunch pails down from a shelf in the refrigerator and opened them. John, a fifth-grade boy, was asking for a snack since he had left his lunchbox on the bus. Other fifth-graders had given him a snack but they had none left to give and he had fared poorly for lunch at that.

Jerry and Jay each had an extra sandwich. "What do you have to trade for a sandwich?" asked Jay as he brandished a left-over baloney sandwich.

"Let's see what's in my pocket," said John as he hurried over to Jerry and Jay. He emptied his pants pocket in front of them. Out tumbled a pocket knife.

"Wow!" exclaimed both boys in unison as they saw the knife fall to the ground. "We could trade for your knife!" said Jay hurriedly, hoping John was far hungrier than he acted.

"I don't think you have enough for my knife," said John. "I tell you what!" added John. "I'll give you a yo-yo for both of your sandwiches," said John.

"Let me see it, John," said Jerry as he set his lunch pail down to examine the yo-yo.

Jerry wrapped the string around and around the yo-yo and slipped his finger into the loop at the loose end of the string. Jerry tossed the yo-yo out and into the air as he waited a moment to jerk gently back on the string and went on see-sawing the yo-yo up and down on the string.

"Let me have a chance to work it," demanded Jay as he stepped next to Jerry and stuck out his index finger for Jerry to slip the loop of string onto. Jay gently tossed the yo-yo out and away from him at a downward angle in a vain attempt to imitate his older brother. Jay slowly wrapped the string up around the yo-yo and tossed the yo-yo down again in another attempt to copy his brother. Again, he failed miserably. Having the patience of a small boy, Jay took the yo-yo back over to John. "What else do you have to trade?" he asked.

"I thought Jerry liked the yo-yo," said John.

"He did, but we do things together, don't we, Jerry?" asked Jay with his open-eyed innocence.

"Yes, Jay, we do," assured Jerry as he looked to John to see what else he had to trade.

"Well, I have almost a full book of matches," said John as importantly as he could. Jerry and Jay both knew they were not allowed matches. Dad would get the razor strop down for sure if they took the matches and were found out.

"Okay, we'll take them for one sandwich on one condition, won't we, Jerry?" said Jay kind of cautiously.

"Well, what's the condition?" injected John as he looked longingly at Jay's sandwich.

"Yah, Jay," added Jerry. "What's the condition?"

"The condition is that you do not tell our sisters about our trade," answered Jay to the relief of Jerry and the understanding of John.

"Okay, you've got a deal!" exclaimed John as he extended his hand, book of matches included to Jerry for safekeeping.

"Hey," said Jay in disappointment as he put his hand back down by his side.

"Look, Jay," said Jerry as John left with Jay's sandwich half eaten after he had turned around.

"We have matches! We better take care of them. If we don't, Dad will whip us for sure. He seems to always find out what we do."

"Yeah Jerry, but we'll keep quiet about this and John can be trusted to keep quiet too."

Jerry pocketed the matches after he checked and found that several matches had been struck and were no good. This practice was also wrong noted Jerry. Matches had to be removed from the book before they were struck! Jerry and Jay went about their recess and tried to forget about the matches so they wouldn't get caught with them. The bell rang again as a tireless reminder to the boys that fun was over for a while. Jerry and Jay went back to their desks in the middle of the other students doing the same.

Science and spelling would be the fare for the end of the day. If any time remained, Mrs. Starry would read to the whole schoolroom of students. She was reading *Tom*

Sawyer! Jerry and Jay always got caught up in *Tom Sawyer*. They felt cheated that they had only a lake to explore and Tom had had a whole river! Tom's adventures felt immediate to the boys, not something from the past.

"Students!" alerted Mrs. Starry. "You will notice that during recess time I laid a test paper on each of your desks. These tests are to show me some of the understanding you have for science. The test on your desk is appropriate for your grade. If you think that you have the wrong test for you, please raise your hand, and I will come to you to see what you think is amiss. So, please check the test you have first. It should state the grade level on the cover."

Mrs. Starry had all of the tests placed properly since there were only twenty-four students in the school in all eight grades.

"Mrs. Starry," said Jay gently with his hand high in the air.

"Yes, Jay?" returned Mrs. Starry.

"I must have the wrong test on my desk. I don't remember having learned anything that's on the front page," said Jay almost pleadingly. The other students looked pale as they too, scanned the cover of the exam.

"Jay. The first page is a general cover page that all copies have. No one has had exactly that material," explained Mrs.

Starry. "But you shouldn't have a test, anyway, Jay. First graders don't get one of these tests. You may give yours back to me, thank you, Jay." The test was not Mrs. Starry's creation but one administered nationwide in an attempt to ascertain student learning relative to other students in other districts.

Jay gave it back instantly. He wasted no time in giving up a test.

"Students! All look at the cover page," said Mrs. Starry. "The front page is just a condensation or summary of all the class levels for science. It does not pertain to anyone in particular and is made to decorate the exam booklet," added Mrs. Starry. "Yes, I know. It looks as if it is an exam page the way it is laid out, but that is just done to catch your eye," said Mrs. Starry as she finished discussing the cover sheet and noting that it had at least caught their eyes!

"Now, let's get back to the exam, shall we? I have to get on with this part of the day's teaching. You all have an exam test booklet and an exam answer sheet, right?" asked Mrs. Starry. All heads nodded in unison, except for Jay. He was the only student in the first grade.

"Read the instructions before you start your exam. If you have trouble with these instructions, raise your hand and I will get over to you to help."

Jerry was still reading his instructions at this point. He, too, understood what was expected of him.

"When you are finished, please bring your exam booklets and answer sheets up to me. Place your booklets on this pile on the left-hand side of my desk and place the answer sheets on the right-hand side of my desk. Before you hand in your answer sheets, make sure that your name and test number are on them. This will ensure me that you had the correct exam for your grade level. This is a final checkpoint for me," explained Mrs. Starry further. "Jay?"

"Yes? Mrs. Starry," returned Jay.

"Jay, come up to the table and we'll go over next Monday's reading class while the others take their exams." And so they did. The exam time went slowly by and Jerry was almost the last one to hand in his exam papers. When he did hand it in, it was a sheepish act laden with insecurity, as it was with many others.

The day was finally winding down as the last of the students handed in their exam papers. "Okay, students," said Mrs. Starry. "All test papers are handed in. Let's clean up the desks, tables, and complete any daily chores you were assigned on Monday. These things need to be done before you can be dismissed to leave for the day and, in this case, the weekend. We have no time for spelling class today or for the story I'm reading."

Jerry and Jay hurried with their chores so they would not be late or look out of place and arouse suspicion. Funny how one has to think when he knows he is doing wrong.

Teachers are good judges of character and Mrs. Starry was no exception. "Jerry and Jay!" she said abruptly as she noticed both boys sitting instead of doing their assigned tasks.

"Have you started your assigned work, yet?"

"We are done already," said Jerry as he stared back at Mrs. Starry with guilt ready to burst cross his face.

"How can that be!" demanded Mrs. Starry as she looked amazed to realize that it was true. *Something is amiss here*, she thought to herself. *I have known these boys too long to believe all is well.*

"Students!" stated Mrs. Starry. "Stand by your desks to be dismissed." Students hastily finished putting away their books as others finished with their chores and stood by their desks as they were instructed. "You are dismissed!"

Some students got books out of their desks to do homework for Monday's classes as others just left the classroom and headed for the cloakroom and others just headed outside.

The bus was waiting as the first students left the schoolhouse. They called back to the others to let them know the bus was waiting. The bus made several trips to deliver students to their respective homes after school, keeping to the same routes as in the morning. Six children got into the car with the bus driver for each trip, so it took only three trips to get all students home since some walked and some parents picked their children up from school on Fridays. Jerry and Jay were on the second trip with their sisters and two neighbor children.

The boys talked softly to each other on the way home. Usually, they made as much noise as any other child, but not this afternoon. The car headed south towards the lake as it left the school. Down the hill it went with the driver, a large and older man, hardly noticing anything but the road. He had driven this route so many times that driving it was automatic to him. The lake sparkled in the late afternoon light as the sun hovered just over the trees on top of the ridge to the west. The lake had a horseshoe-shape to it. The car was heading toward the left or east end of the horseshoe. The road from the school approached the lake just at the bend of the shoe.

"We catch our crawdads here!" said Jay as they traveled over the place where the road greets the lake at the lake's last big bend. During some springs the March wind blows the water against the road incessantly and erodes the road base away. The spring runoff also adds to the lake's water volume. This forces the traffic to take the northern route to and from school.

"We catch great sunfish and bluegills here too," said Jay in an unusually subdued manner. (This was before the lake had been poisoned by the DNR in 1959 to make it a game-fish lake. It was easy to catch twelve-inch perch and ten-inch sunfish and bluegills.)

The boys continued to talk nervously on their way home, trying to fill up quiet and empty minutes with chatter so they wouldn't be forced to endure the quiet moments with thoughts about their deception of their parents and family in their secreting away the matches won with their Mother's added sandwich.

The car/bus went up the big hill, past the store on top, around the corner, up and over a small hill by the townhall and into their driveway. "Good bye! Have a nice weekend," toned the children.

"Thank you. Bye," returned the bus driver as he drove away up the hill and out of sight on his way back to school to pick up the last load of children.

"We have to do our chores, Jay," said Jerry as they made their way to the house. "Then we can look at our matches."

"Brownie!" chimed all of the children as the family pet appeared from under the porch. That he was named by small children was evident at his appearance. The dog was all black except for a brown patch over one eye and long brown hair on the lower and back part of his legs.

The boys did their chores of carrying in water from the well house that was out back of the main house, one pail for drinking and one for cooking. The communal dipper's bowl floated the dipper on the water's surface in the pail. Any slop that ran into a five-gallon pail under the sink from the chores Mother and the girls did in the kitchen had to be removed.

The five-gallon pail had to be carried back to the far end of the property and dumped.

Typically both boys carried this together, each holding on to a side of the bail handle of the metal pail. There was no running water in the house and no septic system for waste water.

"Jay!" admonished Jerry. "Don't slop the pail around. You'll spill the slop on the matches in my pocket and get them wet!"

"Golly, Jerry. I almost forgot about the matches," fibbed Jay as he realized that thinking about the matches made him forget that he had to keep his mind on what he was doing.

The girls had to help Mother with cooking and setting the table. The dishes were typical giveaways (dishes that came in oatmeal and detergent) with country scenes on them.

Knives, forks, and spoons were a jumble of whatever had been available from other sources at one time and all mismatched together to form an eclectic set that fit the basic needs of the family. Whenever the table was set, the tableware pattern was ignored. One person's knife might match someone else's fork, which may match another's spoon, but each had a knife, fork, and spoon. The same was true of the water glasses that sat in front of each family member.

Dad came home and cleaned up from the day's work as everyone got ready for supper. Dad worked in the woods cutting, measuring, trimming, and peeling poplar trees for pulp for a man who owned the rights to cut trees down in the national forest.

Dinner consisted of home-canned venison and green beans reheated and with fresh potatoes. Canned berries were for dessert. There was no freezer for the safekeeping of food, so Mother canned everything.

"How was your day?" Dad asked of the boys.

"It was fine," burst out of both boys together.

This made Dad wonder if all was well with them. He eyed them suspiciously as the family ate supper in silence for a moment.

"How about you girls?" asked Dad. "Did you have a fine day too?"

"Yes, Dad, we did," answered Sherry, the eldest.

"We all had testing during the last part of the day" piped in Liddy, the younger of the two daughters.

"Mrs. Starry gave Jay a test too," added Sherry. "He thought the cover was part of the test and he knew he never saw any of the information contained on the front page. Everyone enjoyed the panicked look on his face before Mrs. Starry told him the test was not for him."

"What happened to Jay's test?" asked Mother as she got caught up in the conversation.

"He made Mrs. Starry realize that the test was not meant for him, so his test was taken from him," said Sherry. "He also made her realize that other students were confused with their test booklets. The cover had things on it that we never had. It even had a chemistry lab on it and many students didn't recognize it," concluded Sherry. "How was your day, Dad?"

"My day was fine," stated Dad. "I got a lot of trees cut, limbed, measured, and peeled. It may have been my best day in the woods! I ended up with two hundred and seventy-eight sticks peeled by the end of the day. The bark comes off the trees so easily this time of year with the sap rising in them. It won't be so easy in a month or so," said Dad thoughtfully.

Cutting, limbing, measuring, and peeling meant that a tree was sawn down with a gas-powered saw, the limbs were removed with an axe or power saw. (Dad used an axe. There weren't many men better with an axe than Father and using an axe saved gas money.) The tree was measured out with a marking stick that was eight feet four inches long, and the "stick" was peeled; it had its bark removed. Dad got twelve cents for each stick he finished. So he had a "thirty-three dollars and thirty-six cent" day. Not bad!

"Oh, Dad!" said Mother. (Mother called him Dad in front of the children.) "A few days like today and we'll have money enough for material so I can sew the children's back-to-school clothes for the fall. Our oldest daughter is in need of some grown-up things soon too," said Mother happily.

Jerry and Jay ate in relative quietness further arousing Dad's suspicions. He said nothing about it hoping the boys would give themselves away in conversation. Not trusting themselves, they remained silent for most of the meal. Besides, small boys eat a lot of food and this in itself demands relative silence.

After the evening meal, the girls cleared off the table and washed and dried the dishes. The boys got to sit by Dad in front of the television set as Dad watched the evening news. They knew that they had to remain quiet as the news was on. After the news, the TV was turned off and Dad went next door to visit his parents. The boys waited to go outside to play until after the girls had the dishes done. They emptied the slop pail once again and made sure enough drinking water remained for the evening. Then they went far enough away from the house so as not to be noticed by anyone.

"Did you bring the small pail with you, like I asked you to, Jay?" asked Jerry.

"Yeah! Jerry, I did" was Jay's answer. "What do you need a silly pail for, Jerry?" returned Jay.

"We, Jay. We need the pail for our fun tonight," said Jerry as he gathered dry grass and some sticks together. Out came the matches as Jerry knelt on the ground next to the pile of grass and sticks.

"We are going to practice making fires, Jay," said Jerry. Jay's eyes got really big as he leaned in closer to Jerry as Jerry lit the pile in front of him.

"Wow, Jerry," said Jay as Jerry lit the pile and the fire quickly consumed the pile of grass and sticks. The fire tried to spread out beyond the pile as Jerry quickly turned the pail upside down over it and smothered it before it got away from the boys.

"Let me start the next one, Jerry!" exclaimed Jay as he tried to pull the matches away from Jerry.

"No, Jay. Not 'til you watch a few more times and learn how to start and smother the fire," added Jerry. Jerry had learned in third grade science that fires needed oxygen to burn and that removing oxygen would put out the fire.

Jay watched patiently as Jerry made, lit, burned, and smothered several more small fires.

"It's my turn, Jerry," whined Jay as he held out his hand for the matches.

"Not tonight, Jay," answered Jerry as he turned toward home, keeping the matches secure from Jay. Jay was too young to trust with matches. Jerry knew this and would not let Jay use them until Jay learned respect for them. Jerry probably didn't realize that he, too, was too young for matches.

It was starting to get dark as the boys got home. The yard light was on, casting it's light out from the house ending with about a twenty-five-degree angle in shadow on either side of the light when compared to a half circle.

The boys went to the well house and rinsed the pail out with fresh water. They had to turn the pump on to do this causing the house lights to dim ever so slightly as to be unnoticeable to most people. The rinsed pail was placed upside down to drain on a shelf in the well house next to a water dipper. The boys closed the door as they left.

Dad waited patiently in the living room as the boys finally made their way into the house.

"Are you still watching TV, Dad?" asked Jerry as he made his way into the living room.

"No. I switched to reading about an hour ago," replied Dad. "Did you have to run the well pump a few minutes ago, boys?" asked Dad as he still feigned interest in his book.

"Yes, we did, Dad," returned Jerry, looking for a place to sit just out of sight of Dad so he wouldn't be seen as he answered Dad's questions.

"Come over here and sit, son, so I can see you," ordered Dad.

Jerry's heartbeat quickened as he began to leave his chair of comfort behind.

"Start getting ready for bed, children," commanded Mom, unaware of the conversation between father and son.

"Go ahead, son. Do as your Mother asked," finished Dad as he went back to his book. Dad knew instinctively that something was amiss with his boys. He also knew that he would be made aware of the discord in due time, so he re-interested himself in his book.

Jerry felt a wave of relief go coursing through him as he realized how close he came to getting grilled by Dad. Jay had not gotten any inkling, yet, of Dad's curiosity concerning them.

Saturday went much the same as Friday night for the brothers. They finished their chores before heading out in midmorning. They had learned long ago that work came before play because it already gave a deeper sense of satisfaction knowing that the work was done and would not crop up at another time to interrupt them. This allowed the fun to advance a few degrees in intensity. Jay learned how to build and put out fires over Saturday.

Jerry was an able teacher. Sunday evening followed by Monday morning school would come all too soon.

"We have to go to church tomorrow, Jay," said Jerry as he got into bed. Jay was beaming as he went over all he thought he had learned over Saturday. He, too, was ready to get to bed.

"Good night, Mom and Dad," said both boys as they got onto bed and pulled the covers over their bodies.

"Good night, boys," chimed in Mom and Dad as they went to bed. It was Saturday night. A while after the family said good night and settled down to sleep, *Jay began to dream. He dreamed that he was a firefighter. He alone was a master at extinguishing a fire. He would be the chief in no time! Fire was no match for him! He could not be burned! He rescued more people than any two other firefighters together. Smoke swirled around as Jay made his way to the burning house. "Get a hose in there!" he commanded pointing at a doorway as others made their way to his position.*

"It's gone, Jay," said his commander. "Just make sure all people are out and safe."

Jay quickly turned to the burning building's occupants and asked if they knew that all people were out.

"We're not sure" was the answer given.

"I'll have to check myself," stated Jay as he made his way into the building. Smoke billowed around him as he pressed onward. Flames licked at his clothes and boots, but he continued in his quest for survivors. The heat was almost unbearable, but onward he went!

Movement towards the left caused him to turn and notice a child crying in the corner of the hallway. Quickly and instinctively, he made his way to the child. He called out for others and, hearing no answer, picked up the child and exited the building. All people cheered and called his name, "Jay, Jay, Jay," as he was clear of the building. "Jay, Jay, Jay," he continued hearing as he woke up startled!

"Jay, Jay, Jay," whispered Jerry as he gently shook Jay. "Wake up and stop talking. What are you thanking people for, anyway?" asked Jerry.

"I was the best firefighter in the world, Jerry!" whispered Jay as he looked around himself just to make sure he had been dreaming. It felt so real to him. "Jerry, the building was on fire and I saved a child. Everyone was cheering. I was a hero. My boss was thanking me. It was great!"

"Jay!" said Jerry softly. "Calm down. It was only a dream. You're not a hero. You didn't save anyone either. It is just your imagination like it is every night! I know 'cause I can't get any sleep 'cause of your imagination!"

"You shuda seen it! It was grand!" finished Jay as Jerry cut him off.

"Jay, get back to sleep. Dream about somethin' else. Somethin' calmer so you don't wake me up!" demanded Jerry.

"Okay," said Jay half-asleep as he fell back on his pillow.

Morning came with the subtle sounds of Dad and Mom walking around downstairs. Daylight was new for the day as Jay got out of bed, removed his pj's and slipped on his shirt and pants. His socks and shoes were put on next as he began talking to Jerry. Jerry just waved him off as if to say *I'm not ready to get up yet. You kept me up half the night.* Jay went downstairs as he called out to Mom and Dad. "I was a firefighter in my dream. I saved people from a fire. Everyone was proud of me." Jay did not realize that this would cause his parents concern.

"Have you been studying about fires in science or have you been reading about fires and firefighters in reading class?" asked his Dad as he watched Jay closely.

"No," said Jay as he continued explaining how he saved the day and became a hero. "I just dreamed it" was his answer.

"Are you sure some other class wasn't learning about firefighting at school, son?" asked Dad as he tried to understand why a small boy would suddenly dream about such a thing if his interest hadn't been piqued by some outside mention of fires.

"Maybe I heard some other class learning about fire, Dad," lied Jay as he slowly woke to the world around him. *I wish Jerry was here,* thought Jay as he wondered what he would be asked next.

"Good morning, Mom, Dad, and Jay," said Jerry as he noticed a strange look on Jay's face. "When is breakfast, Mom?" asked Jerry.

"I'm getting it together soon, son," answered Mom as she continued her task of getting pans out for breakfast.

The girls were soon down and helping Mom with the morning meal. The table was set with eggs and pancakes and homemade jam and jelly.

"Good morning, Jerry," said Dad as he gave up on his questioning of Jay for now. "Your brother was a hero in his dreams last night."

"He was!" exclaimed Jerry. "All I know is that he kept me up most of the night by talking in his sleep. What did he do that made him a hero?"

"He was a firefighter. He saved a bunch of people from a fire, I guess. Everyone thought he was a hero," explained Dad. "What do you think would make him dream of fires in his sleep," asked Dad of Jerry.

"Well, Dad," said Jerry slowly as he thought of an answer that would fit the story. "I think he must have heard about firefighting in school. It must have been from a class Teacher taught."

"Mrs. Starry taught," corrected Dad.

"Yes, Dad, Mrs. Starry taught," agreed Jerry. "We can hear every class that gets taught, Dad. Sometimes we hear things we remember later, but we don't remember where we heard them," finished Jerry, or so he thought.

"I always figure that when a young boy, such as Jay has a dream about something new, it must have been a thing he heard others say or do," explained Dad. "Small boys have great imaginations, but they usually need input to come up with something new."

"Jay is just overactive, I think, Dad," Jerry added, hoping to sidetrack Dad. Dad was hard to sidetrack. You may think you have fooled him; however, he may just be letting you have enough time and words to implicate yourself.

"Enough talk about fires and firefighting," said Mom. "It is time to wash your hands and eat before breakfast gets cold."

Mom always won the day with a meal. Everyone forgot the topic for the mealtime and ate what Mom had made.

The whole family ate breakfast together. Light chatter was heard.

"It's time to get ready for church," Mom said as she picked up the breakfast dishes. "A new pastor will be preaching today." A different preacher may be at church each Sunday. It was rare to see the same one more than two Sundays in a row. Not many people showed up for church, and of those who did, not much money was collected. Unfortunately, money seemed to be the driving force behind religion in this small town. Dad did not go to church with the rest of the family. He usually went fishing. He may or may not be home for dinner.

If he was not home by dinnertime, the family ate without him. Dad worked at least six days a week. He believed Sunday to be his day of rest. He saw no better way to rest than to go fishing.

The church was small. It had fold-down seats like those of a theater in the back and handmade pews towards the front. Up front in the far left-hand corner of the church was a full-sized oil painting of Jesus with royal-colored robes and outstretched arms that hung downwardly, palms up, beckoning little children to "come unto" him. The speaker's podium sat upon a raised area much like a stage. The reed organ was on the left-hand side just ahead of the painting of Christ. An elderly neighbor woman from town or a lady traveling with the itinerant preacher played the organ. A wood-burning stove sat just before the raised area and on the right near the second entrance/exit, its stovepipe slowly rising to a ceiling thimble close by. The painting was the part of the church that seemed out of place.

It was much too beautiful for a country church, even though it seemed at home in its place on the wall. It had a radiance about it that actually drew little children to it in awe at its bright colorful splendor. Christ's halo was so brightly painted that it radiated an almost pulsing light from itself. It had been painted by a man from the neighboring town as a gift to the community. The organist sat at the organ and played whenever the minister nodded at her.

The Sunday service began with prayer. The new minister was dressed in a black pinstripe suit, a starched white shirt, and spit-shined leather shoes. A bible graced one hand as the other reached towards heaven as he spoke. The sermon was about parental authority. It warned children to obey their parents. "Never lie to them but honor them as you would honor the Lord" were his words. The minister also added a little hellfire that seemed appropriate for most boys.

Two boys stared straight ahead as they sat on the fold-down, red-violet covered seats. They didn't dare look at each other or anyone else. They feared others would see the deceit that covered their faces since they each could see it in the face of the other. The sermon went on and on as the minister seemingly attempted to sweat the devil out of the boys. This was probably the first sermon the boys had fully heard.

The sermon ended with another admonition to the children to honor and obey their parent. A prayer was again offered up to God. A basket for a collection was passed around by male ushers who advanced a row at a time only to stand stern-looking at the center aisle end of each row of churchgoers.

Parents watched in knowing sadness as the minister eyed the small monetary amount rendered unto the Lord. They thought by his disbelieving look that he would not be seen again at the small church and that another minister must be sought after and begged to come and preach. Thus was the religious teaching given to all who attended.

"What a Friend We Have in Jesus" was the last hymn of the service. It seemed to give the two brothers a chance to loosen up a bit and helped them lose the pallid plastic face that adorned the space between their hair and their chin.

The minister was the first to leave the church, but, much to the dismay of the two boys, he stopped at the church entranceway and wished everyone a good week as he shook each person's hand as all left the church. Much to the chagrin of the boys, the minister also told the churchgoers that he would see them next Sunday. Mother was ecstatic when the minister mentioned being back next week. No other preacher had ever given that promise to come back.

Jerry and Jay were full of real concern. The same preacher two weeks in a row might mean they would have to take this religious stuff seriously.

Mother went back to the minister and asked him if he and his traveling companions would please come to dinner after services next week. The boys found it hard to breathe as they heard Mom's request. But they were more mortified when they heard the minister say that he and his traveling companions would feel honored to have dinner with the family next week. The boys decided they would run home ahead of the rest of the family.

The boys had their clothes almost changed as the girls and Mother entered the house.

"Don't go running off right away," said Mother to the boys. "I have dinner in the oven and it will be ready soon." The boys thought they smelled baked chicken as they finished changing their clothes before the girls came up the stairs to change their clothes.

"Okay, Mom," answered Jerry as he slowly went downstairs with Jay close behind him.

Dinner went fine as the brothers ate their fill and helped clear the table. The sisters did the dishes as usual while the boys got more water from the well house about seventy feet away from the back door of the house. The boys bought the two pails of water into the house and set them down on the counter.

"Now don't go and run off right away, boys," said Mother. "We will need another pail of water within five minutes. You might as well stay and get the next pail of water before you run off and dump the slop water, too."

"Okay, Mom," chimed the boys.

They soon finished their chores and got ready to go fishing off the pier on their Grandpa's land. They got the cane poles down from under the eave of Grandpa's garage. They knew they did not have to ask Grandpa for the use of the poles; he had already told them to use the poles whenever they wanted as long as the poles were put back where they belonged when they were finished with them. They dug up some worms in the area of the garden where the mountain ash tree provided shade. Worms were plentiful in the normally shaded garden area. They left the shovel standing in the garden just as they had found it.

They got a fish stringer, some extra hooks and went back into the house to get more water before they went fishing. Jerry made sure he had the matches with him as they began to make their way to the lake.

The trail to the lake went across Grandpa's small field; down the hillside at a slight angle; and horizontally through a slightly swampy area; past the ice-skating shanty; and finally to the pier. Ordinarily, the wooden boat would be by the pier. Today Dad was using it.

He could spend all day on the lake whether the fish were biting or not. He was optimistic enough to believe that the fish would be biting somewhere on the lake. He just had to find that "somewhere." Jerry and Jay learned a long time ago that you never went fishing in a boat with Dad because he was a patient fisherman unlike small boys and he stayed on the lake for hours.

The boys laid the cane poles down parallel to the pier. Jerry pulled some brown grass together in a pile, got the matches out, and tried to light the grass to make it burn. It just smoked a bit and went out. He tried once more with the same results and gave up.

"It's no use, Jay! Everything is just too wet down here to catch the grass on fire," said Jerry as he kicked the grass around to make it look more natural.

"Let's just fish for a while, Jerry," said Jay as he grabbed his cane pole and the worms. So the boys fished the day away.

Dusk time was near, so the boys decided to go back to the house. Dad was not in sight yet and they knew better than to yell for him to see if he were close by.

"We're home!" yelled both boys as the back door slammed shut.

"Did you see your Dad?" asked Mom.

"No. Mom. We did not," said Jerry as he got ready to clean the fish.

"Well, get cleaned up for supper after you have cleaned your fish, boys," said Mother as she sat with a bewildered look on her face not knowing if she should be worried about Dad or not. She finally decided that there was no reason for worry.

The boys cleaned the few pan fish that they caught. On their way back to the house, they saw Dad. He had some big fish on the stringer.

"Wow! Dad! What did you catch?" asked Jay as he stared at Dad's fish stringer with eyes the size as walnuts. "Look, Jerry," said Jay with amazement still showing on his face. "Dad caught a whole stringer of fish, Jerry."

All of Dad's fish were at least ten inches long while most were longer.

"Well, boys," explained Dad. "It's time for you to clean more fish," finished Dad.

Back to the cleaning table went the boys. Dad followed as he told the boys to be careful and to remember to remove the fish heads just behind the gills so the fish would not be so small-looking.

"Time to eat," yelled Mom.

"We'll be there soon," called Dad as he turned and walked slowly to the house. "The boys will be along soon, Mom," said Dad. "They just got more fish to clean.

"Someday, Dad, the boys will be too big to clean the fish you catch too!" advised Mom as she kept busy finishing up with meal preparation. (This happened on a day when Dad and a neighbor caught two gunny sacks full of crappies for the boys to clean. They talked to Dad after that and each agreed to clean the fish he caught.)

Supper went fine as the boys and Dad told of their day's fishing. The girls just sat back smiling in disbelief as each story went floating past them.

Evening dishes were washed by the girls as the boys waited while watching the evening news with Dad. Soon dishes were done and the boys finished up their meager chores. Out the door they ran as Mother called after them.

"Boys! Don't stay out late tonight! I want you in bed by nine o'clock!"

"Okay, Mom," answered the boys.

The girls and neighbor children also appeared outside as a game of tag was organized and a person to be "it" was chosen by a majority of the kids. The fastest runner was picked to be "it" first. This left the actual "picking" up to that person since they could catch whomever they wanted. The game of tag was played mostly within the shine of the yard light, which also included some of the yard of the property east of home. The kids had a couple of hours of fun before Mom called for her four to come in for the night. Goodbyes were spoken as all children went home and the four went in the house for the night. *Tomorrow was school again* was the thought that was on the mind of each child.

"Sherry! Get up or you will be late for the bus again!" screamed Mom up the stairs as the other children were almost ready to get on the bus.

Down the stairs came Sherry as she calmly said, "I am ready for school already."

"I have your lunch packed too," said Mother. "You are too late for breakfast, though."

"I don't need breakfast," said Sherry as she left the house to wait for the bus.

The bus came and off to school went the children. Mrs. Starry and one other busload of children were already at the school. A fast game of work-up was being played before school began. Off went the bus driver for another load of children.

The day began as every other day. The bell rang and in came the students. Softball equipment was put away until recess time and everyone got ready for attendance. Once again Mrs. Starry went through each student's name for attendance. It was a good lead-in for the rest of the day. Everyone knew what to expect from the daily routine and that gave its own comfort. The Pledge of Allegiance was recited and a few songs were sung.

"First grade please come up for class," said Mrs. Starry as school continued for another day. "We are ahead of schedule, Jay," said Mrs. Starry. "But we'll keep ahead of schedule with your classes until something goes wrong elsewhere. This way I can bypass your reading class if I have to. Have you gone ahead in your ABC book?" asked Mrs. Starry.

"Yes, I have, Mrs. Starry," replied Jay as he opened his book to the proper page. "I am two parts ahead in my book."

"Sections or chapters," said Mrs. Starry. "We call them sections or chapters in your book, Jay. I am glad to hear that. We may cover both today, if you feel prepared and the class goes well for you."

The class went well and the teacher was pleased that she had two classes worth of time "banked" up if she needed them. Each grade was brought up front for class at the table in front of the classroom. It was recess time before anyone knew it.

First graders don't get picked for softball so Jay went into the wood pile along the south side of the schoolhouse and continued on the fort he was making there. He had hollowed out a fair-sized "room" in the pile and was working on a second room. The rooms were open to the sky but small boys still see them as rooms.

"Jay, find an older boy for me, please, and ask him to ring the bell for the end of recess," asked Mrs. Starry from the open schoolhouse window by the wood pile.

"Okay, Mrs. Starry," said Jay as he climbed out of the wood pile. Off ran Jay to the outfield where he saw a sixth-grade boy. "Mrs. Starry asked me to find an older student to ring the bell for the end of recess. Can you do that?" Jay asked.

"Sure, I can," replied the older student.

Off he went to ring the bell as the game continued. *Ding, DONG, ding, DONG* went the bell as the student kept ringing the bell. Soon all of the students outside were in for classes and the daily classes continued.

"First grade, please come up front for class," commanded Mrs. Starry as Jay got ready for arithmetic. His book had numbers in it, but he had only begun to add and subtract single-digit numbers. Soon all arithmetic classes were finished.

English and social studies (history for some grades, current events for others) went without incident.

Lunchtime was next in the course of the day. Certain children were ready with the teakettle used to wash the students hands. Hand soap was given at the next station. A rinse station cleaned off the soap, which left the drying station where paper towels were used for hand drying.

Milk that was taken cold from a refrigerator was made available before students picked their lunch pails out of the refrigerator. Students usually ate at their desks unless it was an unusually warm day; then they were allowed outside to eat. Today was not hot enough for outside eating.

The work-up game of softball began where it left off from the end of the morning recess. Some students went up into the tannery to walk and talk. Jay went back into the wood pile to build his fort. The fort was taking shape. Two rooms were visible as was a short and narrow walkway between them. The rooms were deep enough to allow Jay to remain unseen except from the schoolhouse window as he worked in his fort.

Jerry played work-up since he was a third-grader and able to catch and bat fairly well.

Mrs. Starry liked lunchtime too. It allowed her time to correct papers from homework or just to stay even with class work of the day.

The bell rang for the end of noon-hour recess. Jerry had gone quickly to the boys outhouse just before the bell sounded. Jay noticed something strange behind Jerry as he walked past Jay.

"Jerry," said Jay as Jerry walked past the wood pile and making Jerry jump as he looked around to find the direction of the voice. Jay again asked, "Jerry, what do you have hanging out of your back pocket?"

This time Jerry recognized Jay's voice and the location of the voice. "I don't know! What's hanging out of my back pocket, Jay. I don't usually look at myself there," answered Jerry as he tried to turn around and look at himself from behind. He kinda resembled a dog slowly chasing his own tail.

"It looks like toilet paper, Jerry," said Jay as he still stood up on some wood to make him see above the wood pile. "Why do you have toilet paper hanging out of your back pocket, or is it paper you forgot to throw away, Jerry?" asked Jay since he was at a safe distance from his brother.

"It's paper we may want to use at recess time," explained Jerry as he pocketed the paper back down into his pocket.

"What do you want to use it for?" asked Jay with a puzzled look on his face as he wrinkled up his nose.

"Don't worry about it, Jay," said Jerry while he finished pocketing the paper into his back pocket as he went around the corner of the schoolhouse and into the school.

Okay, thought Jay as he climbed out of the wood pile and went around the corner of the schoolhouse and into the school.

Science class was next on the agenda of the day. All classes went smoothly as the last recess of the day approached.

"Students! Get ready for recess," commanded Mrs. Starry as she surveyed the room for any unacceptable behavior. Seeing nothing untoward, she dismissed the students for recess.

"Jay," whispered Jerry as he left the schoolhouse and continued around the corner of the building and next to the wood pile.

"What do you want, Jerry?" asked Jay as he got ready to enter the wood pile again.

"Jay, let's find a place to use our matches this recess," said Jerry.

"Okay, Jerry. Where do you want to go?" asked Jay back.

"Not too far, Jay. We have to get back after recess is over," added Jerry.

"Follow me, Jerry," said Jay as he turned slightly sideways and continued in his previous direction. "We can play here and no one will see us," said Jay.

"Okay," said Jerry with a smile as he followed Jay.

"I got the toilet paper at lunchtime to help start a fire," said Jerry as he unrolled the paper from his back pocket and fluffed it up while putting it into position. "Help me get a few small sticks over the paper as I get our matches out, Jay," asked Jerry as he squirmed for the matches.

"Okay, Jerry, I have the paper fluffed up and four sticks over it. I think it's ready," added Jay.

"Wow, Jay it looks good. I taught you well," said Jerry as he gave himself a sideways compliment for training his brother. "Here goes, Jay," said Jerry as he struck a match and held it to the toilet paper. The paper was especially dry since it had Jerry's body heat on it for over an hour. The fire leaped into being instantly as soon as the match touched it.

"Wow!" said Jay as the wood sticks over the paper caught on fire.

"I smell smoke," yelled an older student as he began walking past the wood pile. "Oh no!" he continued. "It looks like someone has started the wood pile on fire! Quick!" he yelled to the boy next to him. "Get a few pails from the cloakroom and some more help. Fill the pails with water and get the water out here as fast as you can before the fire gets away from the wood pile and onto the school."

Off went the student who took the order.

"Who's in the wood pile?" demanded the older student. "Come out now!" he further demanded. Out came Jerry and Jay with sheepish looks on their faces.

By this time Mrs. Starry had heard the yelling as did everyone else in and around school. A small crowd had gathered as Jerry and Jay descended from the wood pile.

"Boys! What have you done!" demanded Mrs. Starry too, as she assessed the situation unfolding before her. "Jack, John, and George, you keep fighting the fire, but be careful! Some of you older boys help bring the pails of water," said Mrs. Starry, as she turned to the other students watching too close to the wood pile. "The rest of you students get down to the ball diamond, now!" she yelled. Off ran the students to the ball diamond as they turned to peek over their shoulders at the chaos going on around them.

"Jerry and Jay, you go down to the ball diamond too with the rest of the students," Mrs. Starry yelled again.

Jack, John, and George had set up a long three-man bucket brigade from the corner of the school while other boys filled the buckets with water to fight the fire. Jack had smelled the smoke early enough for the boys to put it out before it consumed too much wood or got to the schoolhouse.

"How are you doing, boys?" asked Mrs. Starry as she saw the fire slowly give up its life and get reduced to a small spiral of smoke.

"We have the best of it, Mrs. Starry," answered Jack as he kept dumping water on the area still smoking.

"Thank you, Jack for noticing the fire before it got too big to deal with," said Mrs. Starry.

"You're welcome, Mrs. Starry," said Jack while he dumped the last of the water needed to extinguish the smoking area of the fire.

"Try to enjoy what's left of your recess, boys," said Mrs. Starry as she turned toward Jerry and Jay who were looking sheepishly down at their shoes as the other students aimed unfriendly words at them.

"Enough of the jeering," said Mrs. Starry. She went over to both brothers, grabbed each by an available ear and marched them into the schoolhouse. "What were you doing with matches? Where did you get them? Why were you in the wood pile of all places? Don't you know you could have burned down the school and possibly have burned some students in the process?" said Mrs. Starry as she explained the possible consequences of their behavior.

Jerry and Jay stood speechless looking at their feet as the possible repercussions of their behavior finally sank in. They remained mute as Mrs. Starry released their ears and sat at her desk. "I don't know exactly what to do with you, boys," said Mrs. Starry. "But you can be sure that your parents will hear of your reckless behavior!"

"Golly, Mrs. Starry," said Jerry. "We didn't think we would hurt anyone or burn anything down. We were just trying to see if we could start a—"

Before Jerry could finish, Mrs. Starry interrupted him. "Jerry and Jay. It may be best if you just sit quietly in a chair at the table while I think of a proper punishment for you. The boys sat down gingerly and remained quiet as the teacher sat at her desk obviously in deep thought.

"Boys!" blurted Mrs. Starry. "You will not go home on the bus today. I will drive you home. I need to talk to your mother today."

Jerry and Jay looked at each other in wonder and disbelief.

"Boys! Put two chairs up by the blackboard facing the blackboard. Sit down on a chair and do not move!" said Mrs. Starry. She decided that she had enough and would put a stop to their day.

After recess was over, Mrs. Starry decided to conduct classes for the rest of the students. When she finished that, she decided to relax by reading *Tom Sawyer* to the students.

Jerry and Jay would not be able to hear since Mrs. Starry read toward the classroom and not toward the blackboard. Both boys ached to hear about Tom and Huck but each knew this was part of his punishment.

"Students! Do any chores you are scheduled for today. Not you, Jerry and Jay," said Mrs. Starry as she turned to see both boys sliding off their chairs. "I'll get someone else to do your chores today. I want you two to stay right where you are until I take you home."

The boys were taken home to their mother and she learned of their reckless behavior.

"Their dad was suspicious of their behavior all weekend," said Mother to Mrs. Starry. "I just thought he was being too harsh with them. I see now that he was right! He will not be surprised, but he will be stern!"

Dad was stern! When he came home and heard what had happened at school that day, he asked several questions. "How did you get the matches?"

"Well, Dad, we traded a sandwich for them with an older student. He had left his lunch pail on the bus by mistake and had no lunch for the day," said Jerry. "Jay asked John what he would trade for a sandwich after we found that John had left his lunch pail on the bus," finished Jerry.

"Boys," said Dad. "You took advantage of a boy who had no food for the day. Why couldn't you simply have given him a sandwich?"

"Yes," said Mother. "I gave you each an extra sandwich for the day. Did you actually need it or did you try to trick me, too?" asked Mother.

"Oh, no! Mom!" said Jay. "I didn't know John would need a sandwich the morning you made us an extra sandwich for lunch. It just happened that John asked others for a sandwich and I heard him. I asked him what he had for a sandwich, you know, to trade," finished Jay.

"Yeah, Dad," said Jerry. "Jay asked John what he had for a sandwich."

"Don't think that you had no part in this, son, just because Jay asked for a trade," said Dad matter-of-factly. "You had a decision to make. You could either go along with the trade as you did, or you could have stopped the trade since you are the big brother," added Dad.

"Where did you learn how to use matches?" asked Dad.

"Dad, we kinda learned that from you," said Jerry slowly as he lowered his eyes.

"You use matches when you smoke," said Jerry.

"So I do," said Dad. "You realize that you are still responsible for some of the things you do at your age?" inquired Dad.

"Responsible?" said Jerry. "Does that mean we should know and do what is right because we get punished if we don't?"

"Yes, Jerry. It may mean that," answered Dad. "It also means we do what is right because it is the right thing to do. It also makes us feel good that we did the right thing. Why did you start a fire in the wood pile of all places?"

"I built a fort in the wood pile, Dad," said Jay. "We built the fire in the fireplace in the main room of the fort."

"How did you start the fire?" asked Dad.

"I guess I got paper from the toilet at lunchtime for us to use to start the fire, Dad," said Jerry.

Jerry and Jay did get punished. John's parents were contacted and told of the incident just because they were parents too. They needed to know what their child was involved in since he traded the matches to the boys. Mrs. Starry was told of the punishment given to the boys, and that John's parents had been notified. There was no monetary loss or the boys would have had to work that off. She was satisfied and gave no further punishment except that Jay had no more fort in the wood pile.

"I'm glad it's over with, Jay," said Jerry.

"Yeah! Me too!" said Jay.

"School will be done for the year this Friday and most of the kids will forget our fire by the end of summer," said Jerry.

One could tell that the boys were still children since they had no idea of the memory older students have.

SCHOOL SURPRISE

It was a late fall day. A bit of snow lay on the ground. Children laughed and wrestled about in the fresh snow in the early morning schoolyard. Older children were engaged in snowball fights and were trying to put snow down the backs of still other children just talking to friends. If one were to view it from a distance, it would appear to be a scene of happy pandemonium! Children ran and wrestled about in all directions.

Bob saw it first!

"Liddy! Did you see anything short running on four legs?" asked Bob.

"No, Bob! I didn't! And quit trying to scare me!" said Liddy as she looked all around and behind herself. "What did you see, anyway?"

"I'm not quite sure yet that I saw anything. It just seemed that something short and long, and on four legs ran behind the building. I only seemed to see it as it was almost hidden by the building," Bob said as he, too, looked all around himself just to be sure that nothing was close to him.

"What are you talking about?" said Harry as he walked across the sidewalk and into the conversation. Bob explained just what he thought he had seen to Harry just as Mrs. Kroger came out of the schoolhouse. Mrs. Kroger was new to the students this year. One year five different teachers taught at the school. This was good for some students. A new teacher meant much of one's behavioral "slate" was clean again.

"Students! Since I see that all of you are here at the front of the schoolhouse, come in for the beginning of classes," Mrs. Kroger explained.

The students went into the school, and took to their seats as they did every school day.

"We have seen something big walking around behind the school, or at least Bob has," said Liddy to Mrs. Kroger as she went self-consciously into the schoolhouse. Already the story changed in its retelling.

"I am your teacher for this year. My name is Mrs. Kroger," said the teacher as she turned and wrote her name on the blackboard in neatly drawn letters. "Some of you are still calling me your previous teacher's name. I am Mrs. Kroger. Now Students, let's get ready for attendance and then the Pledge of Allegiance before we take the day any further this morning," said Mrs. Kroger. "Morning attendance will help me to learn all of your names too," she added.

After this, she explained the rules she expected all students to comply with as she was their teacher. Attendance was taken, the pledge was recited, and classes began as they had for years long since forgotten at the school.

Jerry raised his hand. Mrs. Kroger nodded her head. Jerry got up and walked to the back of the classroom to go outside to the toilet. As he walked past Bob, he heard Bob saying, "Pssst! Pssst!"

"What do you want, Bob?" asked Jerry.

"Didn't you hear about what we, I mean I, saw before school started this morning?" asked Bob in a whisper.

"No! I didn't!" stated Jerry. "And I don't want to hear it now either," he finished as he went to the cloakroom for his coat and went out the door.

Jerry went around the corner of the building, crossed the length of the schoolhouse, down the hill, past the swing set, and finally into the toilet that stood next to bushes that led up to the tannery. He finished up what he went there for and made his way back to the school without incident. He put his coat back on its hook and went back into the classroom.

"Jerry!" whispered Bob. "Jerry!" whispered Bob louder.

"I heard you the first time!" Jerry fired back in a whisper at Bob. Jerry seemed to be a bit short-tempered with Bob. "I just see no reason to talk to you during class time, Bob," added Jerry. So Jerry went slowly over to Bob's desk watching for Mrs. Kroger to recognize him to give him permission to talk to Bob. Mrs. Kroger nodded at Jerry in approval so Jerry knew that he had permission. "Well, what is so important that it can't wait 'til recess time?" asked Jerry.

"I've been trying to tell you that I saw something big and on four legs this morning just before we came into the schoolhouse for classes," related Bob with added emphasis as he talked to Jerry. "Did you see anything on your way to the toilet just now?" asked Bob with more than just concern in his voice.

"No!" said Jerry emphatically. "Why are you telling such stories, anyway? You know there is nothing like that outside."

"Well, I saw something," said Bob.

Jerry went calmly back to his desk and began readying himself for his first class of the day.

Up went Jay's hand as he waited what seemed like hours for Jerry to return and then for Mrs. Kroger to recognize him. Yes, nodded Mrs. Kroger as she looked up from the class she was teaching and saw the urgency on Jay's face.

Up jumped Jay, obviously in a hurry. He ran-walked past all of the students as he made his way to the cloakroom and then outside.

Phew, he said to himself as he walked around the corner of the schoolhouse and across the length of it, down the hill, past the swing set, and into the toilet. *Golly. I never thought I'd get here!* exclaimed Jay to himself.

Bump! Bump!

"Who's out there?" called a startled Jay from inside the toilet. "If that's you, Jerry, it's not funny," said Jay as he finished up what he had to do. "I'm coming out and you better run or you'll be sorry," he added, wondering if he should really leave the security of the toilet. He heard a rustling noise in the bushes alongside of the toilet and made a mad dash out of the toilet door, across the playground, up the hill, across the length of the schoolhouse, around the corner, and into the school refusing to look back at the origin of the grunting noise behind him. He closed the door sharply with a thud and then hung his coat up on its hook. Into the classroom he strode trying to regain his composure. It was no use. He was as pale as a ghost! All eyes were on him the instant he came into the room.

"Are you okay, Jay?" asked Mrs. Kroger.

"Yah. Sure," returned Jay as he got back to his seat with a soft sigh of relief.

Classes went without trouble and soon it was recess time.

"Students!" said Mrs. Kroger as she stood up front looking at the back of the classroom. "It's time for recess."

Up jumped the students in one body as they raced to the cloakroom, put on their coats, and ran out of the schoolhouse.

Bob grabbed Jerry and Jay as they walked past him. "Did you see or hear anything, Jerry, when you went outside before?"

"How many times do I have to tell you, Bob?" said Jerry almost angrily. "There is nothing out there!"

Bob looked at the powder-white face of Jay as he listened to Jerry. It was impossible to miss the fear in Jay's face.

"What about you, Jay, did you see anything?" pried Bob.

"No!" said Jay hurriedly. "I saw nothing!"

"Okay, Jay. You saw nothing, but your powder-white face is telling me that something happened to you. When you came in from your mad dash to and from the toilet, you looked as if something chased you back!"

A small crowd of students had gathered by the boys as they talked over the happenings, real or imagined.

"Well, Bob," offered Jay, "I got to the toilet okay, but there were two loud bumps on the side of it. I thought it was you, Jerry, so I hollered at you and I heard two more bumps and then some rustling in the bushes."

"Come on, Jay. You know that two of us are not allowed out to the toilet at the same time!" returned Jerry.

"Yeah, Jerry," said Jay, "that thought crossed my mind as I ran from the toilet and back to the school."

"You did what, Jay?" asked Bob as he saw Liddy standing next to him again, her face ashen white too because of the story Jay told.

"I hurried out the toilet door and ran for all I was worth for the school. I heard something grunting as if it were following me."

"Did you see it?" interrupted Bob as he continued his interrogation.

"I'da had to almost stop to turn around to see it," said Jay incredulously. "No way was I gonna do that!"

"Maybe we can track it on the ground," said Bob.

"There is no ground to track on, Bob," said Jerry. "The whole schoolyard is covered in gravel. Are you sure you heard something, Jay, or is it just your imagination again?"

"No, Jerry," said Jay as he pleaded his case like the best lawyer of the day. "I heard something grunting behind me. It must have been almost on my heels."

"If it were on your heels as you say, Jay," said Jerry, "you wouldn't have been able to get the schoolhouse door open before it got you. You better think your story believable before you tell it."

"I think the concrete steps kept whatever it was from gett'en me," explained Jay.

"If Jay is telling something close to the truth, what could it have been?" asked Liddy, her eyes growing larger with every word.

Only four or five other students had heard anything about the four-legged dark animal-thing that now grunted (and was, according to Bob, large) according to Jay.

"A bear grunts," said Bob with an air of authority.

"Oh come on, Bob!" said Jerry, "you know that a bear won't stay around here. If you saw it earlier this morning as you say you did, it would be far, far away by now. It must be something else, like someone's pet or something," ended Jerry. *I'm tired of a discussion that is going nowhere and is eating up my recess,* he thought to himself.

"Hey! Jerry!" said Bob at the retreating figure of Jerry, "we could always start the wood pile on fire if it's a bear. That would scare him off."

"Old, Bob. That's last year's news," said Jerry as he kept on walking toward the ball diamond, not bothering to look back.

Ding-dong went the bell signaling the end of recess.

"Thanks, Bob!" stated Jerry as he rotated on one foot and traced his steps back to the small group of students still trying to figure out what was on the grounds before.

And so classes went on again for the morning. Noon came and went with no other incidents. The last recess of the day was finally at hand. Mrs. Kroger got up from the table where classes were held. She surveyed the classroom and told students to get ready for recess. This meant putting all items that were on top of the desks away. Mrs. Kroger liked everything to be nice, orderly, and clean at all times.

"Jay, put your books away. You are holding up the recess time. Remember, recess time begins when I first ask you to put your things away, not when you leave the building," instructed Mrs. Kroger succinctly. Jay hurriedly cleared his desk so he would not catch the dickens at recess time. Mrs. Kroger learned a long time ago that it was easier to keep control if you allowed students to help keep each other under control, in certain instances.

"Students, you are dismissed for recess," stated Mrs. Kroger as she turned toward her desk and each student raced to be the first one outside.

Most of the snow was gone by now. Work-up was easier to play without snow on the diamond. Most of the students played at the ball game. Each knew he or she needed the practice if the team were to beat Lake Blue School again in the spring. A rivalry had developed between the two schools sometime in the past. No one knew just when it had come to pass.

Playing work-up in the late fall was a gift and every student knew it! Snow usually came midfall and stayed until late April or early May.

"Wanda, BeLinda, and Wil were batting, John was catching, Babs was pitching, and Loren was on first," said George. "The rest of you can remember where you played from each other at the end of last recess. Let's get on with the game before recess is over."

With that, each student went silently to their last position and play began once again.

Jerry had to play second base 'cause he missed the playing at the first recess and lunch got him late to the game. His talking took up all of the time allowed. Playing went from center-outfield, to left-field, right-field, third base, second base, first base, short-stop, pitcher, catcher, and then batter. Sometimes two batters, a catcher, a pitcher, and two outfielders were all that there were to play since there were not enough children to play all of the positions. Sometimes younger students had to be begged to play. Younger ones would only play if they could bat first and then they might quit when batting only got them to distant outfield from a lack of a base hit. Since they usually struck out quickly, they were allowed to make their demands and get away with them.

Ding! Dong! The bell rang signifying the end of recess. The ball game ended abruptly and all of the students went back into the schoolhouse to finish the last of the school day.

Halfway through the last part of the day the temperature began to drop, it began to snow, and Mrs. Kroger turned on the radio. It was an old set that ran by a battery that had a charging system that ran off a small wind generator that sat on a window ledge. The set was horribly out-of-date as were most items in the school, but it still worked well as did the other obsolete items.

There was a loud knocking at the door that bought everyone straight up in their seats. Mrs. Kroger said, "Come in. The door is not locked."

In walked the bus driver as he explained that the school day was over because he needed to get the children home before the snowstorm became too heavy and everyone got snowed in at school.

"All right, students!" commanded Mrs. Kroger. "You all need to put your studies away for the day. Remember, if we have no school, tomorrow, you need to work ahead in all of your classes for Monday. We may have to cover the material quickly too." With that, the students were dismissed and daily chores were left undone this day.

The bus left with the first load of children as the snow fell faster and heavier. Mrs. Kroger had to wait until all of the children were taken carefully home before she could leave.

"I'll take the last bunch of children home, Mr. Brooks," said Mrs. Kroger as she got into her car. The bus already had enough children to fill it as they all waited for the return of Mr. Brooks.

"Okay, Mrs. Kroger. Goodbye and Godspeed on your way home," returned Mr. Brooks as he left with the last bus load of children.

Slowly and deliberately Mrs. Kroger drove the last of the children home. They were children from two families that lived close by the school and each other. This made her decision to help the bus driver easier for her. The snow fell so fast and heavy that Mrs. Kroger had difficulty seeing the road at times.

On her way back, the wind began to blow harder as she approached the road back to the school. She remembered what she had forgotten. *Oh! My goodness!* she said to herself. *I forgot my teacher's guides. I'll need them for correcting papers and to keep ahead of the children.* Up the hill and back to the school she went.

Mrs. Kroger pulled up to the sidewalk in front of the school, opened her car door, and stepped out into the early-winter storm. The wind howled around her and the schoolhouse that sat on top of the hill. The voice of the wind seemed to raise and lower itself as it howled and whistled through the leafless trees and around the building, pushing snow ahead of itself. The snow had a burning sting to it as it brushed across her face. The sun, though hidden by the storm clouds, gave a bit of light to the ending day. The grayness was almost overwhelming. The day itself felt heavy on her shoulders as if a weight had been added to her. The sad and eerie song of the wind filled her head as she fought to make her way to the schoolhouse.

How foolish of me! How nearsighted! I'll be late and my family will be worried were the thoughts she used to chastise herself for her forgetfulness.

Once inside the school building, Mrs. Kroger rushed to her desk, picked up her teacher's guides turned, and noticed that one window had been left open about an inch. She plopped her guides back onto her desk and turned toward the window. A snowy mess was on the floor. As she approached the window to close it, she heard a faint but decidedly guttural noise coming from the outside when the wind died down momentarily and allowed other everyday sounds to be heard once again. Instantly her mind went back to earlier in the day when she overheard some students talking about a four-legged beast. *No! Not beast!* She thought to herself. *I'm hearing things. Next, I'll be seeing things,* she told herself as she took brown paper towels and cleaned up the snowy mess by putting it into the wood box where it would melt and get absorbed by the wood. She closed the window quickly and turned back to her desk.

She picked up her guides and made her way back through the cloakroom, entry hall, and to the front door of the school. She turned the doorknob and hastily opened the door, looked up, screamed, dropped her teaching guides and fell back as the object at the door rushed in.

"Mrs. Kroger!" called the custodian gently as he reached out and caught her before she fell.

"Is something wrong?! Can I be of assistance?" he asked as he saw that she was still limp and not hearing him. Seeing a small chair in the corner of the entry hall, he sat her gently down as he waited for her to join him in the present. She blinked twice.

"I apologize for startling you so, Mrs. Kroger," he replied as he still held her securely to the chair. Slowly she began to respond as she realized that she was safe and no beast was near her.

"Oh, Bill!" she said as she regained her composure. "I thought you were something other than a man."

"But why would you think that?" asked Bill as wonderment and shock crossed his face one after the other.

"I won't bore you with the whole story, but I overheard some students talking about an animal they thought was hanging around the school today and, well, I let an overactive mind draw the wrong conclusion when I first saw you just now. Please forgive me?"

"Oh, don't worry about it. I'm just sorry that I had to be the one to surprise you. And on such a late afternoon as this, yet," finished Bill.

"You can help me, Bill," said Mrs. Kroger. "Give me a hand with my teacher's guides, please. If I can get these to my car, I'll leave. The sooner I get home the better I'll be."

"I'll help you, but tell me more about what the children saw and where they think they saw it."

"Please allow me to tell you the story another day, Bill," begged Mrs. Kroger as she took the last of her study guides from Bill and made her way outside to place them into her car on the floor behind her seat.

""Why, yes I'm sorry for already delaying you in such weather, Mrs. Kroger," said Bill as he followed her out to her car, and turned to leave for his home across the road. "My Mary is not yet back from her shopping trip today. I am beginning to worry about her, too." His wife went to shop at the county seat about twenty miles away this morning and she had not yet returned.

"Well, I'm sure she'll be back soon, Bill. You just need to be patient. Did telephone services get installed in this community yet? I would surely like to call home before I leave this afternoon."

"No, Mrs. Kroger. Telephone services have not yet been installed here. We are told 'next year' every time we write and ask," said Bill.

"Good day, Bill. I must get on my way if I ever hope to get home today," added Mrs. Kroger.

"Goodbye, Mrs. Kroger," finished Bill as he turned and left for his home across the road.

Mrs. Kroger opened her car door and slid onto the seat behind the steering wheel as she instinctively started her car's engine. The engine roared and she put the car into reverse. *Thank God that I have an automatic transmission this time!* she said almost audibly to herself. The car slowly backed up and then away from the front of the schoolhouse as the snow packed tightly under the car's tires. "This is going to be a long drive home," she said softly to herself. "I'll be glad to be indoors again."

Mrs. Kroger turned her car around and then slowed her car down to a crawl as she approached the hill that led down to the county highway. *I'll have to stop at the bottom of the hill at the stop sign to be sure no one is coming,* she reminded herself. No one else seemed to be out on such an evening. She turned left and continued her journey home. The snowing had gotten heavier since she got back to the school a half hour ago. The wind blew hard and then eased up at different times seeming to obey no rules. Snow drifted across the highway in many places so deeply that her car was pulled sharply toward the ditch. She managed to keep it moving steadily along. The county highway was just a glorified path in some places and these places had been muddy ruts in the morning. Now the frozen ruts acted like railroad tracks removing her decision in most steering matters. The heavy snow gave only glimpses of the road and landscape.

Lights seemed to be flashing faintly just ahead of her as she made her way around a ninety degree turn in the road. She leaned on the steering wheel to avoid what turned out to be the county plow truck. Snow flew high above her car in an arch as she slid off the shoulder of the road bed and into the ditch.

The county plow man braked gently as he thought he saw the car he just met slide off the road as he looked in the rearview mirror, waiting for the air borne snow behind him to settle. *Yes. Darn!* said the truck driver to himself as he stopped abruptly in the road and reversed his direction of travel so he would be in position, if needed, to pull the vehicle out of the ditch. *I hope whomever is in the car is all right*, he thought to himself as he backed up slowly. He did not have far to go and he was alongside of the car. He stopped the truck, set the emergency brake, opened the truck door, and climbed down onto the snow-drifted side of the highway. "Hello," he called out as he neared the car. He saw that the engine was still running and the lights were on. "Hello," he yelled louder to get above the noise of the wind.

Slowly the car door opened as it pushed several inches of snow ahead of itself and just as slowly Mrs. Kroger turned and slid off her car seat after turning off the car's engine. "I'm so glad you stopped and turned around," said Mrs. Kroger. "It was snowing and blowing so hard that I hardly noticed you and when I did it was too late to avoid you safely. I felt I had to swerve to miss and my car ended up where it now rests."

"Why are you out so late in this storm?" asked the county plow driver.

"Well," said Mrs. Kroger. "I teach in the next town east and we got the storm news late.

"By the way, my name is Mrs. Kroger. Betty Kroger."

"My name is Ed, Ed Bagely. I've been driving these roads for the county for thirty years. Let me see how far you are in the ditch. Maybe I can pull you out. The sand

I carry in the dumper and the chains I have on give my truck lots of traction," continued Ed as he instinctively made his way down into the ditch. "You went in pretty good!" yelled Ed from the far side of the car. "I think I can pull you out, though." He went back to the truck, fiddled under it, and returned with a cable. "This will get you out in no time, Mrs. Kroger," he said as he disappeared under the back end of her car. Ed hooked one end of the cable to the frame of the car and the other end to the tow hook on the truck. "I'll need you to get back in your car and put it in reverse. I noticed that you have an automatic transmission, so just put it in reverse and try to steer it out in the same tracks you made going in. Do you understand what I am asking?"

"Yes. I do Mr. Bagely," she said as she walked down into the ditch, opened her car door, and slid in behind the wheel. She started her car and gently slid the transmission into R for reverse. Meanwhile, Ed went back to the county truck and slowly drove forward, taking up the slack in the cable until it was taught. He gave the truck more gas as he felt the weight of the car pull back against the truck. Slowly and steadily the car moved as Ed kept the truck moving forward. Ed kept his eye on the car by using his rear-view mirror and when he had the car well onto the road bed, he slowly stopped the truck while watching in his rearview mirror to be sure that Mrs. Kroger stopped her car too. The car stopped leaving slack in the cable and Ed took the truck out of gear, set his emergency brake and stepped down and out of the county truck.

"Mr. Bagely, how can I ever thank you enough for stopping?" asked Mrs. Kroger. "I just chill to the bone when I think of what would have happened if you hadn't stopped."

"Well, Mrs. Kroger, if I hadn't happened along when I did, you probably wouldn't have gone into the ditch," returned Ed as he bent down and removed the cable from her car frame and then the truck's tow hook. "Be careful the rest of the way. You can probably drive on the side that I plowed since no one else will be out. This road hardly gets traffic in this direction anymore."

"Well, I may drive in the other lane at times. I must be close to the river by now. I only have about four miles left to the state highway," explained Mrs. Kroger.

"Yes. It's about four miles to the state highway, Mrs. Kroger. You should be okay then. The county has several trucks keeping that highway open this night," ended Ed as he waved, stepped back up into the truck, and drove off.

Mrs. Kroger turned the car's heater up to high now that she had gotten wet from being out in the snow a bit. She shivered as she put the car into gear and slowly drove off. Over the bridge she went and around the last corner before the state highway would come into sight. A pleasant sight it was too. She saw a county plow truck approaching from the north as she stopped at the stop sign. *Good!* she thought as she slowly turned south onto the state highway. *The county will be plowing just ahead of me all the way home from here*, she thought.

Mr. Kroger had the driveway plowed as he watched at the window since he heard the county plow go by. Into the drive came his wife's car with her in it. Mr. Kroger met Betty at the door. "You must have had a wild drive," he stated more than asked.

"Why, yes Rob," said Betty with a slightly hoarse voice.

"You seem to be getting a hoarse throat too."

"I got wet sometime during the time I went into the ditch on the county highway and after I was pulled out by Ed Bagley who has worked for the county for over thirty years," finished Mrs. Kroger as she went into the bathroom to shed her wet clothes and take a warm shower.

"I suppose you couldn't call from anywhere near the school to let me know you'd be late."

"No," said Betty softly as she peeked her head around the bathroom door. "No service yet! Bill says every time he writes to the phone company, they tell him he'll have service next year. Always next year! He says he will just quit writing soon. Let me get my warm shower, hon, and I'll tell you about my day if you like," informed Betty.

"I don't believe there'll be any school tomorrow," said Rob as he turned back to the living room and his newspaper. "You should probably not talk too much by the way you sound. Soon you won't be able to speak at all."

Off went Mrs. Kroger to take her shower. Soon she was out and felt better. Her voice even felt better after her shower.

"Oh, it's even easier for me to talk since I finished with my shower, dear," said Betty. "I'll tell you about parts of my day just to get your opinion, Rob. Some of the students were talking about a strange animal around the schoolhouse. One boy thought he saw it before school began today."

"Maybe he just imagined that he saw something, Betty," said Rob as he put his paper away so he could listen better.

"Another boy heard it behind him as he ran from the outhouse back to the school while classes were going on," continued Betty.

"Didn't he see it if it was on his tail?" said Rob.

"Oh, Rob! He's just a little boy. He was scared white before he got back into the schoolhouse. He couldn't bear to look at it. It would have been funny if he hadn't been so scared-looking. No one made fun of him, so something must be going on."

"Don't put a lot of stock into what small boys claim to see or hear, dear. Their imagination is much too active at their age to take them seriously."

"I think I heard it too, Rob."

"Are you sure?"

"I don't know what else it could have been, Rob," said Betty. "I had to go back to the school after I helped the bus driver take the students home. One window was open a bit and had made a mess on the floor. I went to close the window and clean up the mess and I heard a definite grunting sound outside and below the window when the wind had died down momentarily. I could not tell what it was, but I know it was something."

The weekend passed with everyone digging themselves out of the snow that had fallen. School was not held until the following Tuesday since the county and towns got behind in their snow removal as the storm had intensified on Friday. Bill had shoveled all the necessary trails clean of snow before school began again on Tuesday. The short driveway, the sidewalk, trails to both restrooms, and a trail to the well pump were all clear of snow as the first busload of students appeared at the school. The school door was not locked and there was a fire burning in the stove. "Good morning, Mrs. Kroger," said each student as each entered the schoolroom after dropping off their boots, coat, mittens, and head covering in the cloakroom.

"Good morning," replied Mrs. Kroger to each in their turn as she stood by the school house entrance. She admitted to herself that she felt a bit spooked when she was alone in the building. She didn't know exactly why, but felt that she was being watched, which made no sense to her since logically an animal outside could not see her when she was inside. All students came inside and took their seats to begin the days learning.

"Good morning, Bill," said Mrs. Kroger as she turned to enter the room behind the last student to enter. "Students," said Mrs. Kroger calmly, "we need to come to an understanding about a rumor going around the school. I have heard some of you talking about a strange animal being present on the schoolyard last week."

"Did you see or hear it too, Mrs. Kroger?" asked Bob hopefully.

"As a matter of fact, Bob, I did hear it last week on the first day of the snowstorm."

"Well! Didn't I tell you so!" blurted Bob to the other students. "I knew I saw and heard something."

"Please allow me to finish, Bob. I will tell you what the animal is."

"How do you know?" asked Bob quietly so he wouldn't seem to be interrupting Mrs. Kroger.

"Let's look at our evidence, shall we? First, I heard that someone, I think maybe you, Bob, thought he saw a low, dark, four-legged animal as it disappeared around the corner of the building."

"Yeah! You bet I did," agreed Bob anxiously.

"Hush, Bob, and I will solve our mystery. The next information came from, I believe, you, Jay. You evidently heard a couple of thumps on the toilet wall while you were inside. Then, you thought you heard a grunting sound behind you as you ran swiftly back to the school."

The other students laughed a bit at the picture that was painted in their mind.

"Well. I didn't know what it was and I was running too fast to turn around!" muttered Jay as he tried to explain away his apparent cowardice of the previous week.

"That's okay, Jay. Most of us here would have done the same thing if we were in your shoes. I also believe that the mystery animal left no apparent tracks in the gravel. Is that right, Bob?"

"Golly, yes, Mrs. Kroger, it is!" stated Bob affirmatively.

"I heard the grunting coming in the open window when I came back to the school to get my teacher's guides. I went over to the second window on the south wall to close it and as the wind died down, I heard a distinct grunting noise coming from outside." All of the students lower jaws dropped in awe as they heard Mrs. Kroger talking and, to them, confirming Bob's tales of last week.

"Before you all get scared and overexcited—"

"It is too late for that, Mrs. Kroger," said Bob as he looked around at all of the others in the room. "I'm kinda wondering, myself. Could you please hurry up and tell us what you think it is?" asked Bob a little fearfully.

"Well, I was watching just a bit ago as you were all entering the school. I saw Bill outside."

"What's that got to do with anything, Mrs. Kroger?" asked Bob.

"And how come we couldn't see its tracks when we looked for them last week?" asked Jerry.

"Well, the tracks were probably there, but only faintly," said Mrs. Kroger. "All of you students walking in the gravel walk messed up the animal's tracks too." All of the students tried to talk at once each with their own question.

"Students! Please be quiet and let me finish!" exclaimed Mrs. Kroger. "Just get your coats and boots back on and let's go outside!" Mrs. Kroger said with finality.

So all of the students got ready and went outside behind their teacher. As soon as they all got outside and on the front sidewalk that Bill had shoveled out, around the corner came a black animal running fast as it could in the deep snow. Bill was a ways behind.

"Look out!" yelled Bob instinctively as he jumped for the schoolhouse door.

"My goodness!" exclaimed Liddy. "It's just a black pig!"

All of the students laughed as Bob came sheepishly back down on the sidewalk.

"Yes, students. It is a pig!" said Mrs. Kroger. "Now, Bob, considering your last performance where you went from the sidewalk to the schoolhouse door, do you want to rethink about Jay not looking back to see what was chasing him?"

"Well, maybe you're right, Mrs. Kroger. Maybe we all would have done the same thing Jay did," said Bob in an apologetic manner.

"Do you think we should help Bill catch his pig?" asked Mrs. Kroger.

"Yes!" shouted all of the children.

So off they all went helping Bill catch his pig. He didn't need much help for as soon as the pig saw the children running after him, he turned to play.

Once the pig stopped to play, Bill was able to catch him and lead him slowly home. "Bring him back to play with us," some of the children asked Bill as he walked away.

"If you really want him to play with you," said Bill, "he is gentle and friendly. If you don't mind. Mrs. Kroger, I could bring him over at recess time. And thanks, for the help in catching him, Mrs. Kroger," added Bill.

"You are welcome for the help, Bill. I really don't mind if you bring him over some recess time. He seems to be gentle enough. Students, let's get back into the schoolhouse again. I want to go over something with you."

Back into the school they all went. When the last one was in and back in his desk, Mrs. Kroger began to ask some questions. "Did we learn anything about our vision and our memory when it comes to relying on them for factual information?" asked Mrs. Kroger.

"Well," said Bob, "sometimes they seem to be a little unreliable."

"Good, Bob!" said Mrs. Kroger. "Anything else, students?"

"Many of us saw something different too, Mrs. Kroger," said Jay.

"Yes, Jay," said Mrs. Kroger. "Our vision and memory can be unreliable and a few people may see something different. This is a good lesson to learn. If we have time to remember about this unreliability and that we may see things differently than others, it may help us to be more attentive to detail when we look at things. This is also true for our hearing. It can be hard to remember just exactly what we have heard too." ended Mrs. Kroger.

"Students! Let's get ready for classes today," exclaimed Mrs. Kroger. She realized that making a learning experience out of the recent happenings would be better than just telling the children what kind of animal they had seen last week. So, classes resumed.

THE BERRY PATCH

"What a bright day outside," said Mother to the children who listened to her. "I think it is time we go picking raspberries in the patch your dad mentioned at supper last night."

"Wasn't Dad talking about the berry patch he discovered down past the sports area, Mother?" asked Sherry.

"Yes, Sherry, I believe he was. He said it was as he stated 'at prime for picking' since no bears had ruined it yet."

"That's a long way for all of us to walk," added Sherry.

"It won't be more than five miles each way," stated Mother as she began readying for the walk. "We'll need to bring regular buckets and berry-picking containers (metal lard pails that had wire bail handles) with us. Each of us will carry something since I have to also include the lunch I packed for us last night and water."

Mother continued preparing for the berry picking trip. She had put together the buckets and lunch and a water container for the walk the night before. She knew that whatever they picked would maybe be left in the vehicle used by Dad so they wouldn't have to carry the berries back.

Everyone was dressed in long-sleeved shirts and long pants for the picking to help guard against the thorns on the berry plant stems. Off they went with Mother, Sherry, and Liddy carrying the brunt of the equipment. Jerry and Jay carried light-weight picking containers. Out the short driveway and onto the township road they went all excited about the fun they would have picking berries and having a picnic-style lunch. Over the hill by the townhall building and down the other side keeping to the right and down to the road that went past the lake.

"I saw frogs jump into the water as we passed by them!" exclaimed Jay as he went for the water where the frogs entered.

"Jay! Stay away from the lake!" commanded Mother as she tried to be ever vigilant where Jay was concerned. "I don't want you to get wet or to fall into the water, Jay, so, please be alert and try to stay focused on berry picking," finished Mother for a little while. She heard a splash from behind her and found Jay wet up to his knee on his right leg side. "You could have waited a while longer to misbehave," said Mother. "Now I'll have to give you more responsibility for our walk," she told Jay. She gave him extra items (three more berry picking containers) for his hands so he was kept busy. "Is that enough, Jay, or do you need more containers?" asked Mother.

"Why do I have to carry so many berry containers, Mom?" asked Jay rather put out by his added burden.

"You need more to keep you busy as you walk, Jay," answered Mother. On it went with Jay until Mother finally said to him, "Jay, you need to listen to me so we get to the berry patch ready to pick berries. Besides, pretty soon you will be carrying all of the equipment."

"It's too hard to do this all by myself," Jay complained as he struggled with his load.

"If you agree to follow my instructions along the way, Jay, I will lighten your load."

"Okay, Mom! I will listen!" answered Jay as he went to her with most of the berry-picking containers. Mother removed two of the four containers he carried and gave them back to the children from whom she had removed them earlier. Once past the lake, the short road to the campsite presented itself. It was a wilderness site with no electricity and running water. There was a well with a hand pump, but no other water. The pump had a bubbler (drinking fountain) built into it just before the water discharge end.

"Mother, may we go up to the campground and just see if anyone is camping there?" asked Sherry.

"We can, Sherry, but it will make us late for picking berries," answered Mother. So they continued on the road to the berry patch as Mother tried to keep all of the children focused and on task. Next came the cemetery with its fancy-looking fence and gates.

Grandfather had spoken with Jay once that the cemetery had been created in 1908 and all family burial ground had to be given up with all persons transferred to the town cemetery.

The grave with the iron cross as a marker was the first one in the cemetery, even though there were older gravestones marking graves. Grandpa said the older ones had been removed from family plots and brought to the new cemetery. There were other roads that ran off from the road they were using. All roads were graveled or were supposed to have gravel on them.

Some of the roads had much grass growing in the center with two paths for car and buggy tires to follow.

"I have to go potty," exclaimed Jay as he stopped walking, put his containers down, turned aside and did what he had to do. After he finished, he got back on the road, picked up his containers and was off at a trot to catch up to the others. "Wait for me!" he yelled as he ran. "Wait for me!" he yelled again.

"Stop yelling, Jay," said Sherry. "You've already caught up with us!"

"I didn't want to get caught by a bear or something," said Jay as he looked down in humility. (This is a rare moment in a small boy's life when he looks anywhere in humility.)

He was a bit scared to be left behind even a few paces.

Past the road to the fire tower they walked with Jerry and Jay wanting to go there instead of picking berries.

"Mom," said Jerry as he slowed down his walking pace with hopes of visiting the fire tower, "can't we go for just a little while?"

"Boys!" exclaimed Mother as she continued walking past the road to the tower. "We need to keep going to the berry patch so we can pick berries today. If we do other things, we'll not have time to pick berries and walk home before Dad is finished for the day." So they continued to walk for another mile before they headed south on another road.

"How far do we go on this road before we reach the berry patch?" asked Liddy.

"We have no more than two miles until we reach the berry patch," Mother informed Liddy. "Any more questions I need to answer?" inquired Mother as she continued walking to the berry patch.

"How did Dad find this berry patch, Mom?" asked Sherry as she continued walking and stayed even with Mother.

"You know that your dad works in the woods cutting trees down for lumber or papermaking, right?" asked Mom to be sure Sherry was listening.

"Yes, I understand that.," returned Sherry as the "berry march" continued.

"Okay, Sherry. You also understand that the land is in a National Forest. Some man bid on the lumber contained in this section of forest land. That man pays up front for the lumber, which is at a very low price but still a lot of money. Then that man has to find men to cut the marked trees down and prepare them for loading alongside a cut or dug road made into the forest." All children were silent while Mother talked seemingly listening and understanding her explanation to Sherry.

"Mom?" asked Jay.

"Yes, Jay?" asked Mother back.

"Why doesn't Dad just bid on and pay for the trees?"

"Well Jay, Dad has four children to take care of, so he can't afford to bid on the trees," she answered.

"How can the man who bids afford to buy the trees?" Jay added.

"Nice question, Jay," said Mom. "The man who bids on the trees is older and all of his children are already gone from home," explained Mother. "He has the money to successfully bid on the trees."

"What are the marked trees?" asked Liddy.

"The marked trees are those marked with a red ribbon by foresters that work for the Forestry Department. Let's forget about the trees for now," said Mother as she tried to change the talk.

Soon they went past the road to the sports area and then past an abandoned family apple orchard that now grew wild.

"Are we getting close to the berries?" asked a tired Jay.

"Yes, Jay. We are coming to the dug road that leads back to the berry patch." Soon they reached Dad's car parked along the road where there was a small clearing. Here the berry patch loomed over the clearing.

"Let's eat our lunch before we begin picking berries," said Mother. "We don't have a big lunch so we may still be able to work right after eating."

"I need the water before I can eat," said Jerry as he reached for the glass gallon water jug.

"Remember, we all need to drink some water so be sure to drink only a bit each time you have some."

"I want a baloney sandwich!" demanded Jay as he sat down in the grass in the clearing.

"Jay, is that a way to ask for a sandwich?" scolded Mother.

"Please give me a baloney sandwich?" asked Jay.

"It's a good thing that you wanted baloney, Jay," said Mother. "We only have baloney sandwiches as does Dad." Usually they had only venison sandwiches. Baloney was a nice change.

"Why doesn't Dad eat with us today?" asked Liddy.

"Dad eats where he ends up working at lunchtime. He takes his lunch out with him so he won't have to walk back to the car when he wants to eat," finished Mother. All ate their lunch and passed the water jug around except for Jay. She held it for him.

"Okay, follow my instructions," said Mother as she made sure each child had a berry picking pail. Pick around the edge so you don't get lost. "Be careful of the thorns on the berry stems too." So many instructions given so fast. *Will any of the children remember them?* Thought their mother as she and the children began picking.

Picking containers were metal lard pails that had wire bail handles. Sherry and Liddy filled their pails fast and dumped them into the larger pails.

There was a rustling noise in the middle of the berry patch. The noise grew louder and louder. Mother and the children all stopped picking and stood still except for Jay. "That's not funny, Jerry," said Jay as he kept up his meager pace of picking.

"What's not funny, Jay?" asked Jerry.

"That rustling noise I hear isn't funny," explained Jay as he still picked berries.

"Jay, look at us," said Jerry. Jay looked and saw that the rest were still standing still.

"Then what's making that noise?" asked Jay again. Up stood a black bear about a hundred feet away from almost everyone.

"Stand still!" said Mother in a loud whisper. There was another rustling sound coming out of the woods too. It kept getting closer and closer. The bear also heard the noise coming out of the woods as he slunked down and, seemingly fearless, began once again to eat berries. Out of the woods came a loud yelling noise with Dad as the source.

"I thought you would be coming to pick berries today. I noticed a black bear here eating shortly after I arrived this morning. You need to make noise and stand tall to chase them away. He won't be back until I've left later on in the day."

"How did you know that the bear was here now?" asked Mother still a bit out of breath.

"As I was walking out of the woods, I noticed things were a little quiet except for Jay so I figured a bit of loud noise would be a good way to test my theory."

"You had good timing for that!" said Mother rather excitedly as she sat down and caught her breath.

"Bears need to eat a lot before early winter sets in or they won't last through hibernation," said Dad. "Sometimes a young bear like the one I scared out of here doesn't have the fear of man strong enough in him. It may take a few more encounters with him this summer, but we'll make sure we instill it within him," said Dad as he sat down a few minutes with his family. He saw that all were doing well. He stood up a bit later and said, "I need to go back to work. I hope you do well picking. You can put the picked berries in the car. I doubt that the bear will be back here since there are more berry patches around." Off went Dad back into the woods. He worked with his brother so he didn't have to work alone.

"Let's get back to picking," said Mother.

"I have a full pail!" exclaimed Jay proudly as he went and dumped it into a bigger bucket.

"Good work, Jay!" said Mother.

"Yeah!" said Jerry. "We're all on our third pail."

"Be nice, Jerry," said Mother. "At least Jay is still picking."

"Yeah, Jerry!" sent back Jay. "While you guys were all scared of a little ole black bear, I kept on picking." It was true. He kept picking, but only because he knew no better.

Once the large pails were full and all of the lard pails were full, Mother explained, "Let's put all of the pails into the car with the windows rolled down so the berries don't get too hot. "Now all we have to carry home with us is the jug of water." explained Mother as she lifted the jug up for a drink.

The jug was empty! "Oh my," exclaimed Mother. "The water jug is empty."

"What will we do?" asked Sherry. "We still have to walk home and it is quite warm out this afternoon."

"Well, we'll just have to locate the spring that your dad talks about. He says it's on a small animal path just off the roadway south of the small apple orchard we passed on the way here." So off they went, out of the dug road and onto the gravel road they had walked on earlier.

"I'm thirsty," said Jay as he wiped his brow with the back of his hand. "How much farther do we have to go for water?"

"The spring should be just a bit down this animal path off the road," answered Mother. Off the road they went with Mother trying to remember the instructions Dad had given her years before when they walked this road. "I think I found it!" said Mother as she smiled at the children. "We must remember where we found this spring," said Mother again, "so we can always find water when we need it if we're down this way."

"The ground is wet all around the spring," said Sherry as she swept the leaves and twigs out of the spring with her hands so the water could flow clear.

"Let it flow awhile," explained Mother. "We need to allow the spring time to flush itself out before we drink from it."

"The water is nice and cold," said Sherry as she bent her head down to the spring to get a drink.

"Be gentle as you drink so you don't stir up the bottom of the hole," Mother said. "We don't want to make the water dirty for the person drinking next."

"I want a drink, please?" asked Jay, sort of nice.

"Okay, Jay, you get a drink next. I can wait," said Jerry, trying to act like an older brother. As Jay drank, Mother began again.

"Remember to drink in some kind of order and after all of you have had a first drink, drink again. Then I will fill the jug about half full for the rest of the walk home."

As they passed a neighbor farmer's place, they saw his wife outside weeding her flowers.

"Hello!" rang out a chorus from Mother and the children. Mother talked to her for a little while and then went on her way with the children.

"When we get there, can we walk down to the fire tower?" asked Jerry again.

"Not today, Jerry. We can go there on purpose some other day," said Mother, hoping that "some other day" never came. "We have to get home before Dad does."

Just on the county road they turned onto next, Jerry and Jay spotted a skunk waddling along the side of the road. He kept going along as if he owned the road.

"Look at that skunk!" exclaimed Jerry. "He won't leave the road for nothing."

"He has nothing to fear from anything the way he smells," added Mother. "Remember this smell, boys.

This is what I am talking about when I tell you that you smell skunky. We need to just leave him alone, boys." Leave him alone they did. Finally he either reached his intended destination or got tired of the constant talk of young children. He left the road. The children had walked far to the left-hand side of the road to avoid the skunk.

"We have just a bit less than two miles left to walk," informed Mother since the boys seemed to have a wearied look on their faces. "Let's stop a bit for a drink," suggested Mother as she sat down on the roadside bank and pulled the cork out of the water jug. "Let's let the boys drink first," said Mother. "They are the youngest."

"Okay, Mother," answered Sherry. "I guess that makes me last."

"No, Sherry. That makes me last," corrected Mother.

After everyone, including Mother, had a drink, there was still enough for another drink before they reached home.

They finally passed the road to the fire tower. The boys realized that they were actually tired and still had over a mile left to walk. Liddy never complained as she walked along with the others. She accepted what lay ahead with confidence and strength.

Again, the family came to the cemetery and then the road to the wilderness campground. "Can we please just walk through the campground?" asked Jerry.

"No!" said Mom shortly. "We need to get home. I need to fix Dad supper as soon as I get home. We have no time to spare today."

Down the road they walked and began to go around the edge of the lake once again.

"I see frogs!" exclaimed Jay as he leaned far over the edge of the water.

"Jay!" said Mother. "Get away from the water! Now!" Jay tried to wheel neatly around but wavered a bit over the water as he did so, but he didn't fall in this time.

"Jerry! Did you see the frogs?" asked Jay as he rushed over to Jerry. The frogs jumped into the lake and made a splashing sound as they landed.

"Yes, Jay. I saw the frogs on the sinkhole side of the lake," said Jerry as he hoped Mother wouldn't see him leaning over the water.

"Jerry!" called Mother. "Quit leaning over the water."

Slowly Jerry obeyed Mother. He knew that if he didn't, he would get some instruction as how to obey his mother from his father. They trudged back up the hill from the lake side. As they got even with the church, they were close to home, so the boys ran fast and beat the girls home. It didn't matter a lick to the girls if the boys beat them home, but it did to the boys. Soon the girls and Mother popped down to the house. They were home from their berry picking day. The children went to play as Mother went into the kitchen to make something for supper.

Dad soon drove over the top of the hill and into the driveway. "Mom, Dad's home," called the boys from outside as they ran to greet their dad. "Did you see the bear again, Dad?" asked Jerry and Jay in unison.

"No," answered their dad as he took some pails of berries out of the car and into the house where he saw his bride making supper. "You know, I never thought about it, but that bear could have gotten into the car after the berries and wrecked it," said Dad.

"I never thought of it either," said Mother. "I am sure glad we didn't have to carry them home with us after all of that picking. I'll have the girls help me clean them after supper and I will begin canning them tonight. "We had a nice time picking until the bear appeared!" said Mother. "We could have done without that!"

"They were there before us and will be, I'm sure, after us too," added Dad.

Mother and the girls cleaned up after supper while the boys went to the well house to draw water for the girl's cleanup chores. Mother, as she often did, stayed up half the night to can the berries. She often canned over one hundred quarts of many kinds of berries and fruit so we had them for dessert over the long and cold winter. Many other mothers of the settlement did much the same.

NEW JEANS AND THEN FISHING

Mother sewed all of the children's clothes while they were young and she stayed at home. She made dresses and blouses for the girls and pants and shirts for the boys. She even made bloomers for the girls. Once in a great while a few articles of clothing for some children were purchased in town, given from cousins in Illinois or from a great aunt who lived in Milwaukee.

After she began working in the town where Dad worked, she no longer made clothes by hand. She purchased clothes from "off the rack, or through a catalogue." One Friday night Mother and Dad went shopping in town and brought home, among other things, blue jeans for Jerry and Jay.

She told the boys, "These jeans are well made and will last a long time. Please wear them tomorrow when you play. I will be home for a day off work."

It was a beautifully clear day for Jerry and Jay to get away from home to play. They had their breakfast eaten and were outside making plans for a day of play.

"Jay," said Jerry.

"Yes, Jerry?" questioned Jay.

"Jay, we have so many good trees to climb around us, why don't we climb trees today?"

"Which trees do you want to climb?" asked Jay.

"Our neighbor told me about a way he climbs and uses trees in his play. We each need an old pair of gloves, Jay, so our hands will not get hurt climbing the tree branches." Jay went home and when he saw his mother, he said, "Do you have two pair of old gloves for us to wear, Mother?" asked Jay.

"I have several pairs of almost worn-out gloves from your father's work in the woods," answered Mother. "Why do you need them?"

"We are climbing trees and Jerry asked me to get two pairs of gloves for us," answered Jay. Mother went to the box that housed used gloves and took out two pair of them and gave them to Jay.

"Okay, Jay. Here are the gloves you asked for. Remember, they were your father's so they will be a bit large for you even though they did shrink when last washed."

"Thank you, Mother," said Jay as he began to walk back to the tree they assessed for climbing.

"So just what does our neighbor do when he climbs these kinds of trees?" asked Jay as he tossed a pair of old gloves to Jerry.

"I'll show you how our neighbor climbs and comes down from a tree across the road from Grandpa's place," replied Jerry as he pulled the gloves onto his hands as he walked. So off they went to the tree across from Grandpa's place. The tree was a pine tree about thirty-five to forty feet high. Its branches were arrayed around the tree trunk in random circles about a foot or two apart. The outward end of the branches were thick and wide and looked soft to the touch.

"It's gonna be hard to climb with all those branches running around the tree trunk," stated Jay as he stood on the road and studied the tree from a distance and evaluated it for climbing as only a small boy is able.

"I know, Jay," answered Jerry, "but once you get up the tree, you will have a surprise!"

Slowly up the tree climbed the boys, the scent of the pine tree permeating the air.

"How do you do it so fast, Jerry?" asked an almost worn-out Jay.

"It helps me to lean out a bit from the trunk as I climb," answered Jerry. So, a slightly timid Jay leaned out from the trunk of the tree and continued climbing by grabbing the branches about a foot out from the tree trunk.

"Wow, Jerry!" said Jay as he began to climb faster. "It is a bit better."

"It's better because you have more space for your body between the branches," answered Jerry.

"What are we going to do after we climb the tree?" asked Jay.

"Just watch me!" was Jerry's only answer this time as he remembered his neighbor when he told him how to have more fun. Jerry held on to the last branch he had climbed and swung his leg over the branch. He then grabbed on to the branch with his left hand, too. He eased up slightly on his grip and let himself slowly slide down the top side of the branch. His hands automatically caught the next branch down as he slid down from branch to branch. He leaned back slightly so the end of the preceding branch would not slap him in the face as he slid down. Jay followed Jerry's lead as the boys slid down the tree again and again.

"What do you suppose the boys are doing?" asked Grandpa of Grandma as he sat on his chair in his living room, looking out the window.

"I suppose they are doing just what other boys their age do," replied Grandma.

"I better watch them," said Grandpa as he saw the boys climb the tree across the road from his house. "They're sliding down the branches of the tree!" exclaimed Grandpa to Grandma with unbelieving eyes as he got up from his chair. Across the living room floor and through the kitchen raced Grandpa as he grabbed his jacket on his way out the door of the shed and out to his driveway. He was just in time to see a worried-faced Jay lose his grip on a branch and go tumbling down the last eight feet of the tree and fall on his back in the tall grass at Jerry's feet.

"Are you okay?" asked Grandpa as he watched a struggling Jay try to catch his breath. "Relax, Jay!" said Grandpa as he began to chuckle at Jay's antics. "You just got the wind knocked out of you. You'll be okay. (Grandpa had the gift of seeing humor in most anything that happened in life.) You could have hurt yourself doing a stunt like that. Look at your pants!" exclaimed Grandpa to the boys. "Your mom is going to be very upset."

"Why should Mom be upset?" asked a truly confused Jerry as Jay recovered his breath.

"You got pitch from the pine tree all along the underside of your new pants. It is impossible to remove it from your pants. Why is your back pocket locked shut?" asked Grandpa with a knowing smile on his face. Jay was up on his feet reaching for his back pocket as Grandpa spoke.

"Jerry!" shouted a frantic Jay as he tried to get his hand into his right-hand back pocket. "My pocket is stuck shut! Mom's going to be so mad!" As he stood listening to Grandpa explain these things to Jerry, Jay felt the crotch of his pants become stiff and stick together as he tried to walk. He looked down at himself and saw that the pitch had turned a dark blackish brown in color. It stuck the crotch of the pants legs together like glue. He had to swing his hips from side to side to be able to make forward progress. He would have been a strange sight to someone not knowing what was going on with him.

The boys waddled slowly home to where Mother was working to clean house, fold, and iron clothes, and make supper for when Dad would get home. "Mom," said Jerry self-consciously.

"Why so glum?" asked Mom.

"Well, Mom," said Jerry. "We made a mistake with our new pants."

"What do you mean by saying you made a mistake with your new pants? Come in here and let me see you, boy."

Into the house went the two boys. They explained what happened as they showed their new pants to Mother. "Oh, my goodness!" exclaimed their mother. "Whatever made you do such a thing?" she asked in amazement.

Jerry explained to Mom that the neighbor boy told him how he enjoyed his tree climbing by sliding down the branches of pine trees instead of climbing back down.

"I never heard of such a thing!" declared their mother. "Are you sure he just isn't trying to make you do something he would never dream of doing himself just to see if he could get you to do it?"

"I don't think so," said a meek Jerry. "He wouldn't be so mean, would he?"

"I'll find out by asking his mother later on today. You have both ruined your new pants. Go and change into some other clothes so you don't hurt your skin or get pitch on some other items. I'll think of a punishment after I talk to our neighbor. Go play outside."

Mom called the neighbor and found out that her son said no, he did not slide down the branches of a tree after he had climbed one because it sounded too dangerous to him. This happened to be just the answer the boys' mother thought she would receive.

The day was young and already spoiled for the boys, so they decided to change pants and go fishing. Nothing came so naturally to young boys as fishing!

"Grandpa," asked Jay as he entered his grandparent's house. The children nor their dad knocked on the door of Grandma and Grandpa's house. They simply entered slowly. If there was a knock, the grandparents knew someone other than family or neighbors were waiting for them outside.

This also applied to the children's house.

"Hello, Jerry and Jay. What do you want?" asked Grandpa as he turned to the door to face Jay.

"Grandpa, can Jerry and I use your fishing poles when we go fishing today?" asked a downcast Jay.

"Of course, you can!" answered back Grandpa. "Remember I told you a long time ago that you could use those poles hanging under the eave of the garage anytime, just let someone here know what you are doing and where you are doing it so they know where you will be," finished Grandpa.

"Thank you, Grandpa!" said Jay kinda confused as to what he should do before asking Grandfather for the use of his fishing poles. Jay spoke just above a whisper since he was still thinking over what Dad would do when he got home and saw the boys before suppertime.

"We plan on fishing at our neighbors at the end of our road" is what Jerry told Grandfather.

The boys went to Grandpa's garage, reached up under the eave, and took down the long cane fishing poles Grandpa kept there on three sixteen-penny spikes. They checked both poles for line, a hook, and a bobber. Observing that these items were present, they made off to the lake with their can of worms and fish stringer. This day they went to the end of the road to fish off the neighbor's dock. They were known by all people in the settlement and had been given permission to fish from several rowboats that were turned upside down in the grass on the shore of the lake.

The unlocked boathouse had oars and life jackets. The boys had permission to use these items too but would not do so today. Today they would fish off the end of the boat dock. It was mid to late morning when they began to fish. They caught pan fish, which was the only thing anyone caught in the lake. The pan fish were big. The boys had caught perch up to fourteen inches long, sunfish up to eleven inches long and bullheads up to a foot or longer. Usually, the fish were around eight inches long and enough were caught for a meal for the family of six since the fishing was good.

The boys baited their hooks, and carefully swung them into the water out from the dock. They silently noticed the pungent odor of lake water and rotting vegetation around the lake's edge mixing with the sweet smells of late spring blossoming wild flowers and tree pollen. Jay's bobber began to swim around on the water and took a sudden dive out of sight. "Jay!" said an excited Jerry. "Your bobber is out of sight. Catch your fish!"

"Whoa!" said Jay as he quickly raised his cane pole. (If you've ever used one, it is difficult for a small boy to quickly raise a long cane pole). "I missed him!" said a frustrated Jay out loud but to himself.

"Wow, Jay!" said Jerry. "You missed him. I'll bet he was a big one and he ate all of your worm. you have to bait up again." Jay slowly drew the cane pole up and walked it slowly back to the grass where he put another worm on his hook. Meanwhile, Jerry put his bobber just about where Jay had been fishing. Down went his bobber just like Jay's had done.

"Look, Jay!" exclaimed an excited Jerry. "I caught him. Ain't he big!" Jerry caught a big perch about ten or more inches long.

"Wow!" said Jay as he stumbled back out onto the dock and fell into the lake along the side end of the dock near shore.

"Jay," said Jerry, not looking at Jay but believing Jay had dropped his pole in the water "look at my fish. Isn't he great!"

"Jerry," called Jay.

"Where did you go, Jay?" called Jerry.

"I fell off the dock and into the lake. Help me get out!" pleaded Jay.

"Okay," said Jerry as he then noticed a long cane pole in the water sticking way out from the end of the dock. "I see you now." Jerry bent down and, grabbing Jay by his hand, helped him slowly out of the lake. "Jay, how do you manage to keep doing such things as this? Are you just trying to entertain me?"

"Don't be funny, Jerry. I just tripped as I rushed out on the dock to see your big fish. Where is your fish, Jerry?" asked a dripping-wet Jay.

"He's already on the stringer and hanging off the dock edge. What did you trip on?" asked Jerry of a slightly envious Jay.

"I'm ready to catch fish now, so look out, Jerry!"

"I have to look out or you'll knock me into the lake too if I'm not careful," said a laughing Jerry.

Jay slowly flung his baited hook back out into the lake and began to watch his bobber with new determination.

Shortly after his hook floated down, his bobber went under catching him off guard.

"Get him, Jay!" yelled Jerry as he got out of Jay's way on the dock.

"Here he comes," said an ecstatic Jay with a wide smile on his face as the fish turned sideways and put up a great fight. The fish was a sunfish just under a foot long. As they put the sunfish onto the stringer, a muskrat swam by just a few feet away from the dock. They noticed him by the wake left after him as he swam in the water.

"We better see if there's a bucket in the boathouse, Jay. Something might try to eat our fish here if we just leave them here in the water," said Jerry. So, Jerry took his line out of the water and went into the boathouse to look for a bucket. When he came out with a bucket, he met the neighbor just by the door to the boathouse. "Hi, Mr. James," said Jerry. "I just got a bucket for our fish since we see muskrats swimming close to the dock."

"Hi, Jerry," said Mr. James. "Yes, any kind of animal here could eat your fish, even a Turtle," said Mr. James. "Hi Jay!" called Mr. James to Jay as Jay waved a hand in greeting but stayed fishing on the dock. "What's biting? And why are you so wet?"

"Jerry got a big perch and I got a big sunfish, Mr. James," said Jay as he turned to see Mr. James while talking to him. "Oh, and I fell into the lake at the shore end by the dock."

"You boys keep on fishing here. I've got some work to do around the yard today." Mr. James had a huge yard that fronted on the lake. He also had several flower gardens that required much work for them to stay attractive. His yard had many mature trees that required picking up downed branches and also required trimming the grass around them by hand since the mower would not trim tight to the trees.

"Okay. Thank you, Mr. James," said the boys as they concentrated on their fishing and Mr. James went back to his chores happy that the boys were fishing and therefore staying out of trouble for the most part. There was talk that the next spring, the DNR would poison the lake to get rid of the massive amount of pan fish so game fish could be added to the lake since it was hoped that a premiere game fishing lake would be the result in a few years.

"Jerry!" exclaimed an exuberant Jay who just stared ahead at his cane pole, which was bent almost to breaking. "Help me, Jerry, before I get pulled into the lake!"

"Well, Jay," said Jerry, "hold your pole end up and just keep fighting him!" Jay did just that too.

"He's too big for me, Jerry! I can't get him in!"

"You don't need my help, Jay. Just stay with him," finished Jerry. The boys had kind of a competition between them and if Jay lost a big fish, it would be good for Jerry's ego. The fish gave one last great jerk and pulled a tired Jay off his feet and made it appear that Jay just stepped off the dock and into the lake. Jay sank to the bottom as he thrashed around stirring up mud and debris from the lake bottom. Jay felt the muddy bottom squish under his struggling bare feet as he kept a tight hold on his fishing pole. The air began to smell of lake water and decaying vegetation. Jay made more noise than a flock of ducks splashing by a shore line.

Jerry rushed to Jay and grabbed the back of his shirt just as Jay had pushed himself up from the bottom. Jerry slowly floated Jay to the shore on the side of the dock so his feet would touch the lake bottom and he could walk on his own power.

Jay horsed the tired fish into shore and beached himself and the fish on the bank. Jay fell next to the fish he had just caught. Both the fish and Jay gasped for air like two fish out of water. Jay was a little upset with his brother.

"If I hadn't pulled you to shore, Jay, you would be floating around in the water just like your bobber." The fish was a huge bullhead about fourteen inches long. There were no catfish in the lake, so it had to be a bullhead. Once in the bucket, the fish wrapped itself halfway around the bucket as it tried to swim but just splashed Jay with lake water as Jay studied the bullhead.

"He's bigger than your perch or my sunfish," bragged a "puffed up" Jay. He thought he was the better fisherman because of his catch. Jay was entirely wet and full of mud since the lake bottom was full of silt at this end.

"You look like a mudpuppy, Jay," teased Jerry as he kept fishing, hoping to catch a bigger fish than Jay had just caught.

Jay looked down at himself and noticed that he was wet and muddy. The fish he caught had blocked all other thoughts from his mind! "I need to go home and change clothes, Jerry," said Jay as he took inventory of himself and his surroundings.

"You don't need to change your clothes, Jay," advised his older brother. "Just stay fishing and you will dry out in no time."

"What about the mud on me, Jerry?" asked a still-dripping Jay.

"We'll brush you off after you have dried a while," advised Jerry again.

"Okay!" answered Jay. Back to fishing for the boys!

Jay decided that he would fish from shore, so off he went to the left of the dock. There was a small circular pool barely connected to the lake. He noticed something small and roundish swimming on the surface of the pool. As he approached the pool, Jay saw that the round things swimming on the water's surface were newly hatched mud turtles. In some places they are called painted turtles, but we called them mud turtles here. Jay caught one with his hands and saw a yolk sack still hanging slightly down from under the turtle's shell.

These small turtles had just recently hatched!

"Jerry!" called Jay as he caught a second turtle.

"What do you want, Jay?" asked Jerry as he kept on fishing off the dock.

"Come here! You need to see what I found swimming in the pool!" continued Jay.

"All right!" yelled Jerry back as he removed his fishing line from the water and began to leave the dock and walk to Jay. "This better be good, Jay!" exclaimed Jerry. "You took me away from fishing for what?"

"Jerry, I found newly hatched mud turtles!" explained Jay as he kept turning the turtles over in his hand to view their yolk sacks.

"You're going to get 'em dizzy, Jay," joked Jerry as he arrived at Jay's side. "They are neat, Jay. They are just the size of a half dollar!"

"You think Mom will let us keep one in the fishbowl. There are no fish in it since Mom accidentally cooked the last two she bought," said Jay hopefully. It was true. Mother bought two goldfish that she liked, put them in a glass fishbowl and having no other place to put them, put them on the oil burning stove in the living room not realizing that they would slowly get too warm and loose the oxygen from the water and slowly cook. It was a sad morning when Mom got out of bed, began to make coffee for Dad and make breakfast for the family. She had walked into the living room and glancing at her goldfish, saw them floating belly up. She finished making breakfast, but her heart just wasn't in it.

"I remember that, Jay. I hope it doesn't bring back sadness to her," answered Jerry. "I think she'll let us have the fishbowl for that if she'll allow them in the house. We'll have to ask her tonight! Put the turtles in our empty bait can, Jay."

"Jerry. There are another four turtles next to the bank. Can I catch them all?"

"Yeah, catch them all, but I'll bet Mom won't allow any in the house. We can keep them outside in a metal bowl or something."

By now Jay was done fishing. He had better things to do. He bent over the edge of the bank of the pool and, seeing a snake; he jumped with fright and fell right over it and into the pool with a loud SPLASH.

"Jerry," said Jay in a voice as self-controlled as he could manage. "Can you help me get up?"

"Jay!" exclaimed Jerry as he came running over. "You fell into the lake again! That's three times already! You're a walking hazard. I'm glad you are not fishing by me! What were you doing?"

"I was bent over the bank when I saw this snake in the water. It scared me for a minute and I lost my balance and ended up in the pool; I didn't really fall into the lake this time. I fell into the pool."

"They're both the same, Jay! The pool is the lake because the pool is a part of the lake!"

"You won't tell Mom, will you?" asked Jay.

"Jay, you fell into the lake so many times. I don't have time to tell her about all of them!" Jerry was letting Jay know that he wouldn't tell on him but not in so many words. "But you'll need to dry out before we get home so come and fish close by me, but not right next to me by the dock after you round up your turtles!" that was more talking for Jerry than he usually did in a day. So, Jay went over to the pool again and captured his now dispersed "pets" and put them into his empty bait can.

The boys continued to catch fish, Jerry from the dock and Jay from shore. The bucket slowly filled up and off they went for home carrying their prized bucket of fish and Jay's turtles. After seeing their bucket of fish, Mother decided they would have fresh fish for supper. Jerry and Jay cleaned the fish and presented Mother with the fruits of their labor. Dad liked fish and would be pleased. His only complaint would be that he didn't catch the fish himself.

"Mom," added Jay as he presented the turtles for her examination, "I was wondering if I may keep these baby turtles in the fishbowl?"

"Jay," said Mother, "the turtles are wild creatures that are meant to live in the wild. They die easily if kept in a fishbowl. Sorry, honey, but it is best if you return them to the pool you found them swimming around in today."

So, Jay took his five turtles and walked down to the neighbor's property and slowly made his way to the pool that was just barely connected to the lake. He looked for snakes and, seeing none, knelt by the edge of the pool, submerged his bait can with the turtles in it and let them float out of the can and make their way to the shore of the pool and continue their natural existence. His mother had taught him a valuable lesson.

Wild creatures need to stay in the wild for their best life.

WINTER SAILING

It was late fall in the north-central part of Wisconsin in the mid-twentieth century. The small lakes that dotted the landscape for miles around had frozen over as was typical of mid-to-late November. Most of these lakes were spring-fed. Huge underground springs flowed all year and gave the lakes their sparkling clear appearance. They had no inlet; just an outlet that flowed even in the dry summer weather, though the flow was then much slower.

This particular year the lakes froze over before any snow fell, thus leaving a smooth and unblemished surface for all who would use the frozen-over lake for winter recreation. When the snow finally came, as it always does, it blew across the ice into secluded bays and shorelines on the south and eastern edges of the lake. Some rocks and logs that announced themselves above the ice caught half borders of snow as the snow tried to make its escape to the shore.

It was into these surroundings that Jerry and Jay had the good fortune to be placed by God.

Two weeks before this day, Jerry and Jay had been visiting their neighbor who operated a small nursery.

"Doc! Where did you get all of this plastic?" asked Jay.

"The problem I am having, Jay, is not where it came from but where it will all go?" said Doc seeming genuinely puzzled. "But to answer your question, Jay," continued Doc, "I receive many of my seedling trees wrapped in plastic last spring. I did not keep it on purpose. It just seemed to pile up here in the shed when I unwrapped the seedlings before planting them. Although most of my trees come from seeds that I plant from the seed harvesting I do for my seed stock, some are purchased as small trees for planting. There! Did that satisfy you as an answer, Jay?"

"Golly, yes, Doc, it did," said Jay. "Well, if you don't need it, can Jerry and I have some?"

"You may have all you want, but you better get your parent's permission before you take it home," advised Doc as he wondered what the boys would do with all of the plastic, about thirty sheets almost ten feet square each.

"What do we need it for, Jay?" asked Jerry as he looked puzzled at Jay and then at the plastic.

"I don't know yet, Jerry, but I am sure we have a use for it!" answered Jay. "I'll go home and ask Mother if we can have the plastic." Away went Jay out of the yard and up the hill to go home to ask Mother about the plastic. "Mother, Mother," called Jay as he approached the outside door of the house. "Our neighbor has plastic he needs to get rid of and Jerry and I need some for our fun," puffed Jay as he finally made it into the house.

"Slow down, Jay," said Mother as she tried to understand what he was talking about. "Tell me in a calm voice just what you are talking about, Jay."

"Mom, Doc has lots of plastic from seedling trees that he gets in the spring. He has lots of sheets of clear plastic he doesn't want or need. Can Jerry and I have them for our fun?"

"Let me see, Jay. You want to know if you may have the plastic sheets Doc has and doesn't want. Why do you want them?" asked Mother. "And don't you realize that you have to be careful with plastic. If you roll up in it, you may suffocate in it. I don't know, Jay. It could be dangerous."

"We don't know, yet, Mother, just what we'll do with it, but a boy can't get plastic given to him just any day of the week, and we'll be careful with it and not roll up in it or anything," finished Jay.

"Where will you and Jerry put the plastic, Jay?"

"We could put it in back of Grandpa's shed behind his garage. He doesn't use that space," answered Jay.

"Well, Jay. Don't you think you better ask your grandfather if you may use his shed as a place for the plastic before you bring it home?"

"Does that mean we can have it if Grandpa agrees?"

"Yes, Jay. If he agrees," said Mother while she left the room to continue working.

Jay was happy with Mother's limitations. He knew Grandfather would agree to any reasonable request if it were in his power to grant it. Mother knew the same.

"Grandpa!" said Jay as he ran across the yard to Grandfather's house. "May Jerry and I store some plastic in your shed? We can get plastic sheets from Doc and we need a place to store them."

"What's all this noise about?" asked Grandfather in a gruff voice, trying to fool Jay into thinking he was upset about something.

"You don't fool me, Grandpa," said Jay as he approached his Grandfather. "You are trying to make me believe that you are upset, but I know better. You are hardly ever upset." Jay was correct. Grandfather was almost never upset. It took a lot to upset Grandfather since most things, according to him, had humor in them; you just had to hunt for it sometimes and other times you had to use someone else's point of view.

"Okay. You got me there," laughed Grandfather. "You got up too early for me today. Tell me what you have on your mind, Jay."

"Well, Grandpa," Jay explained, "we, Jerry and me, we can get sheets of plastic from Doc. Mother says it is okay to get them if you let us keep them in your shed. Can we store the sheets there, Grandpa?" begged Jay to a grandfather who hardly needed coaxing from his grandchildren, say nothing of begging.

"How many sheets of plastic will you be getting and for what purpose will they be used?" asked Grandfather as he tried to get some information.

"Well, Grandpa, we don't rightly know yet why we need them, but you see, you can't always get sheets of plastic given to you very often, so Jerry and I would like to store them in your shed until we figure out what they are good for. I almost forgot, there are about thirty sheets of plastic."

"How big are the sheets, Jay?" added Grandfather.

"The sheets are about ten feet by ten feet, Grandpa," answered Jay as he squirmed and wiggled as only he could.

"Well, Jay," said Grandfather as he let the discussion linger on, "I don't mind you storing the plastic in the shed. Would you mind if I used a sheet or two myself?" asked Grandfather.

"Oh no, Grandpa. I won't mind. Thank you for letting us store the plastic in your shed. Use as much as you need."

So, it was done. The boys got all the plastic sheets Doc had. They counted twenty-seven in all.

Jerry had "paying" work to do some nights after school. He mowed an elderly lady's lawn in summer and did snow removal in winter for some elderly neighbor in the area so Jay had the time he needed to think up things to make using plastic sheets. He decided he needed some light-weight material for a framework. He found plaster lath that had never been used. Again, he found himself asking Grandpa for something, being pretty sure ahead of time that Grandpa would agree to his request. Of course, Jay got Grandpa's approval. Grandpa also told Jay that he could use any fasteners such as screws, nails and such in the garage. He could use tools too, but they had to be brought back after each use so they would not be lost.

"After all," Grandfather had said, "other people will need to use the same tools sooner or later."

Jay went back down the hill to Doc's house to tell him about the plastic sheets. "Doc, I talked to Mom and Grandpa and they said it was okay for us to get the plastic sheets," exclaimed an excited Jay.

"Okay, Jay," said Doc. "How many do you want?"

"Do you need to keep a few for yourself, Doc?" asked Jay.

"I will be getting more seedlings in the spring, Jay. They, too, will be wrapped in plastic. Besides, I put three sheets aside for use on my windows to help keep the cold out this winter."

"That's what Grandpa was thinking when he asked me if I would mind if he used a couple sheets," said Jay while his thoughts went back to his conversation with Grandpa. "We'll take the rest if you don't mind, Doc," said Jay hopefully.

"You may have the rest, but be careful not to wrap yourself up in the plastic sheets so you suffocate, Jay," advised Doc.

"Jay," said Jerry, "do we need so many sheets?"

"It isn't every day that you are given plastic sheets, Jerry," answered Jay as he kept thinking of ways to use plastic sheets. The boys gathered the large square sheets of plastic, went up the hill, down the other side and into Grandpa's shed.

"Jay, are you sure we can keep the sheets here in Grandpa's shed?"

"Yup," said Jay. "I asked him about it and he said yes. I asked Mom first and she said it was okay if Grandpa let us store the sheets in his shed, so we are okay. She also told me not to wrap myself up in the plastic so I would not suffocate."

"They all say that, Jay, because we are kids and they think we don't know better, but we do know better," finished Jerry.

"I know what I'm gonna make for us, Jerry," said an excited Jay as a grin spread across his face.

"What are WE going to make?" stressed Jerry.

"Okay, Jerry. We are going to make sails for our sleds for sledding in the big bay of the lake," explained Jay. "We need to cut down some of the aspens growing on Grandpa's land by the lake. Grandpa cuts them every few years to help stop their growth. We'll cut them for side poles that we attach the plastic sheets to so the sails can be rolled up when we walk across the ice of the bay and set up to sail!" The boys went down to the lakeshore on

Grandpa's land and began to cut some aspen trees down for sail poles.

"What are you doing?" asked an interested Grandpa.

"We are cutting down poles for our sled sails, Grandpa," answered Jay calmly. "Is it okay that we are doing this?" asked a sheepish Jay as he continued cutting aspen poles for sled sails.

"Well, I don't rightly know, Jay," said Grandpa with a serious look on his face. Jay dropped his axe and stopped cutting and Jerry soon followed suit. Grandpa got the reaction he was looking for so he relented. "You're okay, boys," chuckled Grandpa. "I got you!" he added.

"Oh, Grandpa," said the boys. "We should have known you were joking." The boys attached the plastic sail material to the upright poles using large-headed roofing nails. They put a strip of cardboard over the plastic and then nailed it to the poles so the wind would not strip the plastic through the nails and off the poles in a strong wind.

The following day the boys had off school. It was a cold and windy day, perfect to test their sails. They put the sail and poles onto their sleds along with their ice skates and rode the sled downhill heading west. They pulled their sleds up the hill at the end of the road. Slowly, they made their way to the lake. When they got to the lake, they sat down on their sleds and took off their boots, pulled their skates on and kinda skated across the lake pulling their sleds and sails across behind them. Jerry got across the lake first and got his sled ready. He sat on his sled and popped open his sail. It caught the wind immediately and propelled him forward at a great speed.

"Jay," screamed Jerry against the sound of the wind, "this is amazing!"

Jay sat down on his sled and slowly raised his sail into the wind. Off he went like a streak across the almost clear ice. "Wow, Jerry! This is better than I thought," said an almost-exhausted Jay, trying to control his speed and direction at the same time.

Both boys learned that it helped a lot to hold the sail to the opposite side of the direction you wanted to turn, but not too far. If you needed to slow down, you just leaned your sail forward, spilling the wind and allowing the sled to slow down. The shoreline flashed past Jay as he tried to raise his sail back up so it would again be full of the wind. Jay decided that he wanted to turn to the left since he was getting close to shore.

"Watch, Jerry," screamed Jay as he tried to get above the noise of the wind. Jay put his sail out to the right as he let some of the wind out. It didn't help. "Oh no!" yelled

Jay as his sled did a fast turn to the left, rolling over, and spilling Jay and his sail to the right as he skidded across the ice on his right side and face. He slid about ten feet before he stopped. His face was red and almost had a rash on it. "Ow, Jerry," said a tired and sore Jay as he gathered his sail, got back on his sled and filled the sail with wind again. The shoreline rushed past in a blur as Jay maneuvered his sled gently around log ends sticking up above the ice and around rocks near the shore. "Wee!" said an elated Jay as he sailed past Jerry who was already heading back across the lake to take another trip on the ice.

"Take it easy, Jay," yelled Jerry to his little brother. "There are a lot of rocks sticking up in the small bay. I wouldn't want you to do another face braking." Jay decided he needed to stop and join his brother for another run across the ice, especially now that he understood better how to control his "ice boat." Jerry decided that he would just use his skates with his sail behind him and his arms out on either side of his body. He rolled the sail up a couple of feet before he attempted his new travel mode.

"What are you doing, Jerry?" asked Jay. "Don't hit a crack in the ice, it will send you sliding so you will do a face braking too," teased Jay as he slowly rubbed his stinging face.

"Don't worry about me, Jay," boasted Jerry, sure of himself. Off he went as soon as he opened his arms. The sail filled with wind and he sped across the ice at an extreme rate of speed. He whizzed past Jay in a flash, his face taking the full force of the wind. Jerry turned left and then right as he tried to get command of his ice-skating sail. He stopped short of his sledding distance.

"Why are you stopping, Jerry?" asked Jay. "You have a long way to go yet if you want to go."

"Jay, look at my face. It looks worse than yours with your ice facial."

"At least you didn't fall down," added Jay. Jay got back to their agreed starting point and made another run on his sled. He noticed the plastic sail protected his face from the wind in the high-speed travel across the ice. They both made two more trips on their sailing sleds before they decided it was time to go home. The last trip was the longest trip. They packed their winter boots in front of them on the sled and were off. They sped across the length of the long bay and into the narrows rumored to have been one of the two Native American crossings on the lake.

Later on, the boys showed their winter sails to the neighbor boys and had them watch as they used the sails with their sleds. "I would like to try one with my skates," said Nick.

"They would work great with skates, but if you hit a crack in the ice, you will go sliding across the ice on your body," said Jay. They all used different configurations of the plastic sails over the winter to "sail" on the lake using sleds or skates. Skate sailing proved to be potentially treacherous since, as Jay claimed, getting a skate caught in a crack in the ice would send one tumbling across the ice in unprotected fashion. Great speed could be attained in the big bay of the lake when winter sailing, so sled sailing was the better way to approach the sport.

LONGEST WALK

Mother told me to walk to the grocery store. I was to get milk for tomorrow's breakfast. So, off I went on my way to the store in the tavern that was about a quarter mile away. I was armed with a paper bag and a flashlight.

It was a dark, damp December night. Plump flakes of heavy snow were falling. A blinking red light on a hilltop a mile or more away south of me silhouetted the bare branches of the tall maple trees at the end of our driveway in the front yard. They appeared as giant demonic monsters with uplifted arms and outstretched fingers that poked at me through the red glow of darkness. The slight breeze made the bare branches clack together as one would imagine the dangling bones of a skeleton would do. A ten-year-old sees and hears many things when he is out and alone in a rural area at night.

I made it past the driveway and up the hill to the left, my feet telegraphing my approach to the night as they packed the newly fallen snow with a *crunch* as each footstep connected with the ground. I rounded the corner where one fork of the road slopes down the hill to the lake and the other slope sparkled from tavern lights that advertised to a passerby of beverages and groceries available inside.

I noticed the parking area mostly empty of vehicles as I approached the building. Knocking the clinging snow off my feet, I opened the door and quickly entered. I saw very few people at the bar side of the building, but noticed that all were friendly looking with ready smiles on their faces.

"Hello!" I said as I walked across the floor to the grocery section of the building. I received a chorus of "hellos" back at me, with some questioning me why was I out on such a night. I barely heard this comment over my shoulder as I went to the counter in the grocery side of the store.

"What are you needing on such a night as this, Jay?" asked the nice lady behind the counter.

"I need a gallon of milk for breakfast, Mrs. Folgen" was my direct answer. Mrs. Folgen walked into the back storage area and soon returned with a gallon of milk. I paid the required fifty cents (She rarely charged the fifty-cent deposit on glass jugs, only doing so if one actually broke the jug) for the gallon container of milk and put it into my paper bag.

As I turned around and retraced my steps to the front door, I received several voices wishing me "good night." I called back the same as I opened the front door and made my way out into the dark, damp, and cold still night air. It had quit snowing and the temperature had fallen several degrees. I began walking the short distance to home. Feeling somewhat apprehensive, I began to walk faster as the store lights left an aura in the night air behind me and the red blinking light before me turned the air and night environment to an alternately dull red and starless black as I went downhill and turned the corner, heading west toward home.

Crunch, crunch, crunch went my feet into the still night air. My trudging feet continued to send out a *crunch, crunch, crunch* and my mind said *wait!* I listened closely as I took a few steps. *Crunch, crunch, crunch* I went and stopped. I heard another faint *crunch* after I had finished walking. *This is just my mind playing tricks on me,* I told myself as I tested my theory by taking a few more steps and stopping again. It happened again! I thought I began to hear a faint, short rush of air behind me as if something were breathing in short, excited gasps. Slowly, I reached into the pouch of my parka and my knowing hand found the familiar cylinder of the flashlight I carried. Slowly, ever so slowly, I withdrew the flashlight from the pouch in my parka as I turned my body at my hips equally as slow so I faced almost directly behind me.

Click! A beam of light sliced through the night air. My heart leaped into my throat and a stinging chill raced up my spine as the light revealed an animal resembling an overgrown dog about thirty or so feet behind me. All that registered in my mind were the glowing eyes, slight open mouth with a distended tongue and yellowish white teeth. A slight panic struck me and instinctively, I withdrew and turned off the flashlight, as I had turned back around. I kept my hand on the light as I proceeded slowly on my way home. I imagined the *crunch crunch* of footfalls behind me the rest of my way home and it made the last of my walk an eternity. The *crunch* echoes ended at the end of our driveway where the yard light begins to light up the outdoors.

On entering the house, Mother asked, "Why are you so pale?" I told her and Dad about my walk home, but Dad attributed it to the imaginative mind of a ten-year-old boy.

Early the following morning I related my story to Grandfather. He put on his coat and hat and followed me out of his house. Across the empty space we went and to our house. He checked several tracks in the snow and noted that they were not dog tracks and had to be those of a wolf just as I had suspected. The animal had circled our house, presumably in search of food or me.

A wolf spent most of that winter not far from our house and those of our neighbors.